Ten Commandments in Schools & Sunday Rest by Law:

Advice for Christians in 2025

Table of Contents

Something on the Horizon

In June 2024, the State of Louisiana passed House Bill 71 into a law requiring that the Ten Commandments be posted in all public and State-funded school classrooms.[1] It is the first U.S. State to pass a law *mandating* the display of the Ten Commandments in schools.[2] According to AP News:

"The legislation that Republican Gov. Jeff Landry signed into law on Wednesday requires a poster-sized display of the Ten Commandments in 'large, easily readable font' in all public classrooms, from kindergarten to state-funded universities."[3]

These posters are required to be in place by the beginning of 2025.[4]

As to the exact format of the display of the Ten Commandments in schools, House Bill 71 stipulates the following:

"The nature of the display shall be determined by each governing authority with a minimum requirement that the Ten Commandments shall be displayed on a poster or framed document that is at least eleven inches by fourteen inches. The text of the Ten Commandments shall be the central focus of the poster or framed document and shall be printed in a large, easily readable font.

(2) The text shall read as follows:

'The Ten Commandments
I AM the LORD thy God.
Thou shalt have no other gods before me.
Thou shalt not make to thyself any graven images.
Thou shalt not take the Name of the Lord thy God in vain.
Remember the Sabbath day, to keep it holy.
Honor thy father and thy mother, that thy days may be long upon the land which the Lord thy God giveth thee.
Thou shalt not kill.
Thou shalt not commit adultery.
Thou shalt not steal.
Thou shalt not bear false witness against thy neighbor.
Thou shalt not covet thy neighbor's house.
Thou shalt not covet thy neighbor's wife, nor his manservant, nor his maidservant, nor his cattle, nor anything that is thy neighbor's.' "[5]

As you can see, the Commandments are left unnumbered in the text and are broken across the lines in such a way that they could be interpreted as being either the Biblical or the Roman Catholic version, depending on who is reading it.

Note that, even in the Roman Catholic version, the precept against graven images is still present: It is not that it was entirely taken out, as many mistakenly believe. The problem is that it was *removed as a stand-alone commandment* and tacked onto the very end of the First Commandment, which has the effect of hiding it from view in many cases where an abbreviated version of the decalogue is displayed. This is precisely what leads many to believe that the Biblical Second Commandment was omitted in the Roman Catholic version, and this shows that the change has been quite effective at achieving this aim.

'Virgin Mary and Child' - wooden statue (19th century) with embroidered clothes
- Santa Maria delle Grazie a Toledo Church in Naples" by Carlo Raso. Public Domain[i]

It is important to note, for reasons that will be explained further, that Governor Landry's momentous action of signing this bill into law took place at Our Lady of Fatima Catholic School in Lafayette, Louisiana.[6] This, in itself, should not be surprising, as, although statistics from different sources vary, it is clear that a comparatively high percentage of those in the State who profess to follow the Christian faith identify as Roman Catholic.[7] [8] [9] However, the birth of this new law, which effectively engages the power of the State to enforce the precepts of the Church, taking place at a Roman Catholic school in a largely Roman Catholic State is highly significant in its symbolism.

In its legislation, Louisiana categorizes the Ten Commandments along with other documents that are "historically significant", including the Mayflower Compact and the Declaration of Independence, as it appeals to legal precedents such as "Act No. 602 of the 2006 Regular Session of the Legislature which provided for the secretary of state to publish the Ten Commandments and other historically significant documents for posting in court houses and other public buildings to address 'a need to educate and inform the public as to the history and background of American and Louisiana law'".[10]

This characterization of what is primarily and intrinsically a *religious* document as a *historical* one in the effort to make its promulgation within schools a legal requirement, it may readily be discerned, is intended to sidestep the prohibition in the First Amendment to the Constitution of the United States, which declares that "government shall make no law respecting the establishment of religion"[11] and to which State governments are obliged to adhere.[12]

Similar bills requiring the Ten Commandments to be displayed in school classrooms have been proposed in other States, including Oklahoma, Texas and Utah,[13] suggesting that this is a trend that should be expected to grow.

As justifications for enacting this law, Governor Landry publicly proclaimed that Moses was the original giver of the law[14] and asserted that the United States was founded on Judeo-Christian principles, in support of which he cited a letter purportedly written by James Madison expressing that the future of the United States hinged on the capacity of its people to govern themselves according to the moral principles of the Ten Commandments.[15] However, these statements belie the truth on both of these points:

Firstly, the original lawgiver (in the Biblical context) was God, not Moses. The Former gave the Commandments, and the latter merely relayed them to the people.

Secondly, according to an article in the *Florida Times-Union*, as of 2008 when it was written, no such letter of James Madison that Governor Landry purportedly cited from had ever been found among Madison's writings, although the same quotation from that supposed letter had been recognized for decades by those aware of that fact as a core falsehood underlying what has been deemed "The Ten Commandments Hoax". According to the article, "The false quote itself has been around since the 1950s, but it appears that a 1994 Rush Limbaugh broadcast gave it its current wide circulation".[16]

Assuming positive intent on the part of Governor Landry, it goes far and fair enough to say that he *apparently* took the James Madison quotation at face value without confirming its veracity.

As for the Founding Fathers' actual views on religion as it pertained to the foundation and governance of the United States, their documented actions have spoken louder than unsubstantiated rumors of their words ever could:

A historical fact that Governor Landry is also *apparently* unaware of is that the United States of America, while still in its national infancy, formally and emphatically denied any notion of its having been founded as a Christian nation — when the sensitive question of the matter was evidently raised — at the time of its negotiation of a peace treaty with an Islamic one. The treaty, containing the following clause, was signed by President John Adams in 1797:

> "As the government of the United States of America is not in any sense founded on the Christian Religion,-as it has in itself no character of enmity against the laws, religion or tranquility of Musselmen [Muslims],-and as the said States never have entered into any war or act of hostility against any Mehomitan [Mohammedan] nation, it is declared by the parties that no pretext arising from religious opinions shall ever produce an interruption of the harmony existing between the two countries."

> —*Treaty of Peace and Friendship between the United States of America and the Bey and Subjects of Tripoli of Barbary: Article 11*[17]

Even certain of the Founding Fathers who outwardly displayed affiliations with Christianity still reflected peculiar unorthodoxies in their worship. Primary examples of this are seen in the religious practices of George Washington and Thomas Jefferson:

Washington, who is known to have been an Anglican[18] who regularly attended church, usually got up and left just before the communion service began.[19] It should be pointed out, here, that the Anglican view of communion, or the Lord's Supper, rejects the Roman Catholic notion of the transubstantiation of the bread and wine into the literal body and blood of Christ.[20] Therefore, it cannot have been an objection to that notion that was his reason for having regularly excused himself from taking part in the sacrament, unless he actually misunderstood the Church of England's position on it. It seems more probable, to this author, that what in the Lord's Supper his conscience could not abide was the spiritual acceptance of the whole Word of God and the atoning blood of Christ's sacrifice that the bread and the wine represent to Christians.

Jefferson, who once referred to his personal religion as *Christianism*[21], compiled his own version of the Bible wherein he omitted verses that associated supernatural concepts and miraculous events with Jesus; effectively dismissing the divinity of Christ.[22]

The Founding Fathers of the United States, by and large, are better known for having been Deists and Freemasons than having been Christians. All but five of the fifty-six signers[23] of the Declaration of Independence were, reportedly, Freemasons.[24]

George Washington (1732–1799), President of the United States of America
by arthur.strathearn. Public Domain[ii]

Deism is a rationalistic belief in a Supreme Being and, often, in one who is considered to be detached from and uninvolved in the lives of humans.

Freemasonry is a fraternal society that, notwithstanding the differences between its two branches, the Scottish Rite and the York Rite, universally recognizes as the Supreme Being the so-called "Great Architect of the Universe" (GAOTU) and esteems as one of the "three great lights of the Lodge", along with the square and the compass, whichever holy book is revered in the religion predominant in the locale, or by the presiding Master, of each lodge — whether that book be the Christian Bible, the Islamic Qur'an, the Hebrew Bible, the Hindu Gita, the Mahayana Buddhist Dhammapada, the Sikh Granth Sahib, or the Zoroastrian Zenda Avesta. The only explicitly stated religious requirement for any member (upon joining, at least) is the belief in some Supreme Being.[25] [26]

In his authoritative *Encyclopædia of Freemasonry*, Albert Mackey, a 33rd-degree Mason, explained the significance of the Bible within the organization:

> "The Bible is used among Masons as a symbol of the will of God, however it may be expressed. And, therefore, <u>whatever to any people expresses that will may be used as a substitute for the Bible in a Masonic Lodge</u>. Thus, in a Lodge consisting entirely of Jews, the Old Testament alone may be placed upon the altar, and Turkish Masons make use of the Koran. <u>Whether it be the Gospels</u> to the Christian, <u>the Pentateuch</u> to the Israelite, <u>the Koran</u> to the Mussulman, or <u>the Vedas</u> to the Brahman, it everywhere Masonically <u>conveys the same idea</u>—that of <u>the symbolism of the Divine Will</u> revealed to man. [underlined emphasis added]"[27]

From Mackey's explanation, which suggests that any book regarded as Holy Scripture in any non-Christian system of faith is a suitable alternative to the Holy Bible in a Masonic lodge where that other faith prevails, it becomes clear that the singular and unified Freemasonic concept of the "will of God" entails an amalgamation of the identities of *all of the gods* of the numerous world religions into one. This view squarely contradicts the sovereignty of the God of the Bible and the teaching that the only way to the Father is Jesus Christ.

In her book, *Occult Theocrasy*, published in 1933 after her death, Lady Edith Queenborough (whose given name was Edith Starr Miller), asserted that Freemasonry is controlled by Luciferian Occultism:

"Many authors have published books on Freemasonry, some printing the rituals, some their personal observations on certain facts, but few of these authors, having themselves passed into occult masonry, the real masonry of the Cabalistic degrees which is in touch with all secret societies, Masonic as well as non-Masonic, have been able to state that *Luciferian Occultism controls Freemasonry.*

Though this is indeed the case, neither the President of the Council of the Order of the Grand Orient of France, the supreme chief of French Freemasonry, nor the president of the Supreme Council of Scottish Rites will be received at the meeting of a simple Luciferian ceremony just on account of his title and dignity unless, at the same time, he possesses a diploma of Cabalistic grade which requires another initiation. On the other hand, the first Oddfellow from Canada, a member of the Chinese San-ho-hui of China, a Luciferian Fakir from India, all these can visit at their pleasure all lodges and inner shrines of ordinary Freemasonry in all countries because, in each one of the Satanic sects, the directing authority is exercised by heads who belong to the most exalted masonic degrees of the different rites, degrees which are for them of secondary importance. These chiefs, at the request of their subordinates of the Luciferian societies, deliver to them freely the diplomas necessary to obtain admittance everywhere, as well as the sacred words and yearly and half yearly pass-words of all the masonic rites of the globe. [with a Footnote here referencing 'Bataille, *op. cit.,* p. 36. ', which is a book on occultism by Carl Hackse entitled *Le Diable au XIXe Siècle* (Volume I) that he published under the pen name of 'Dr. Bataille']"[28]

The same spirit of religious syncretism that is propounded in Freemasonry, as will be shown, will be instrumental in drawing together all of the world's people of faith to fulfill what is prophesied in Revelation 13:3-4:

"...all the world wondered after the beast. And they worshipped the dragon which gave power unto the beast: and they worshipped the beast..."

World Interfaith Harmony Week Award photo, Amman, Jordan, on April 17 2016
by Ocaorthodox. Creative Commons Attribution License[iii]

Despite the all-inclusive embracement of the world's various religious faiths, which began within Christianity in the form of ecumenism in the purported spirit of *brotherly unity* and has since broadened its objective to a universal syncretism, these nominally independent Christian denominations and other religions will all still be required to assimilate —in some manner and to some degree— within the fold of the one-world religion of the antichrist; that religion which declares that eternal salvation is reserved only for those who are "in communion" with its particular system and that this can be achieved and maintained only through conformity to its unbiblical dogmas and rituals.[29] [30]

Alice Bailey, a Co-Mason and wife of high-level Freemason, Foster Bailey, with whom she founded the Lucifer Publishing Company, was the leading voice of Theosophy during the early twentieth century and is widely regarded as a founder of the New Age Movement. She wrote numerous books, much of the content of which she claimed was telepathically dictated[31] to her by a Tibetan "Ascended Master" named Djwal Khul.

In her book, *The Externalisation of the Hierarchy*, Bailey wrote of a coming event that would unfold in four stages beginning in the year 2025. Although Bailey conveyed much of her meaning cryptically, through her use of ambiguously general terms likely intended to perplex those uninitiated in her belief system, it seems that she was describing a gradual revelation to the world of the structure of spiritual powers that rule over it. If that is the case, then, given the sympathy for the Devil in Theosophical thought[32] and Bailey's claimed communication with what can be understood from a Biblical standpoint only as a demon or fallen angel, it is clear enough that the ruling hierarchy she referred to is not that of God but of His adversary.

"For we wrestle not against flesh and blood, but against principalities, against powers, against the rulers of the darkness of this world, against spiritual wickedness in high places."

—Ephesians 6:12 (KJV)

Bailey's predecessor in Theosophy, Helena Blavatsky, had openly stated in her own book, *The Secret Doctrine*, that "It is Satan who is the God of our planet and *the only* god".[33]

What is more disturbing is that Bailey equated what has been discerned above as meaning the exposition of the Satanic forces that rule over our planet with "the order of the Kingdom of God":

"...the new world order, the order of the Kingdom of God under the *physical* supervision of the Christ. This might be regarded as the externalisation of the spiritual Hierarchy of our planet. Of this, the return of the Christ to *visible* activity will be the sign and the symbol."[34]

Note carefully how she wrote that "the return of *the Christ* to visible activity" will signify the onset of this new order of things. The term "the Christ", with the definite article, is generally a dead giveaway that the one being referred to is not Jesus Christ of the Bible but, rather, the imposturing *Cosmic Christ* of New Age belief.[35]

Also in *The Externalisation of the Hierarchy*, Bailey revealed that the involvement of *the Church* and *Freemasonry*, and *the educational establishment*, all three of which she stated had already been infiltrated at her time of writing by "disciples" of the powers mentioned above, will be key to bringing about their externalization—this new age, or new world order—that she falsely equated with the Kingdom of God:

"<u>The three main channels through which the preparation for the new age is going on</u> might be regarded as <u>the Church</u>, <u>the Masonic Fraternity</u> and <u>the educational field</u>. All of them are as yet in relatively static condition, and all are as yet failing to meet the need and to respond to the inner pressure. But <u>in all of these three movements, disciples of the Great Ones are to be found</u> and they are steadily gathering momentum and will before long enter upon their designated task."

"<u>The Masonic Movement</u> when it can be divorced from politics and social ends and from its present paralysing condition of inertia, will meet the need of those who can, and should, wield power. It is the custodian of the law; it is the home of the Mysteries and the seat of initiation. It holds in its symbolism the ritual of Deity, and the way of salvation is pictorially preserved in its work. The methods of Deity are demonstrated in its Temples, and under the All-seeing Eye the work can go forward. It <u>is a far more occult organisation than can be realised, and is intended to be the training school for the coming advanced occultists</u>. In its ceremonials lies hid the wielding of the forces connected with the growth and life of the kingdoms of nature and the unfoldment of the divine aspects in man. In the comprehension of its symbolism will come the power to cooperate with the divine plan. It meets the need of those who work on the first Ray of Will or Power.

<u>The Church</u> finds its mission in the helping of the devotee, in aiding the great public which is innately religious and of good will. <u>It hides in its heart those who vibrate to the great love ray,</u>

the second Ray of Love-Wisdom. <u>Christ Himself works through it</u> and by its means seeks <u>to contact the vast Christian public. It is the leaven in His hands to leaven the whole lump</u>, and being in a form comprehended by the people, it can touch the great masses of seeking souls.

<u>By means of the educational work of the world</u>, the Great Lord seeks <u>to reach those of the intelligent public who cannot be reached by means of ceremonial and symbolism</u>, as in Masonry, or by religious means and ritual, as in the Church. It touches the masses and those in whom the intelligence aspect predominates to the lessening of the other two aspects. It aids those men who are predominantly on the third Ray of Intelligent Activity.

<u>In all these bodies there are to be found esoteric groups who are the custodians of the inner teaching</u> and whose uniformity in aspiration and in technique is one. <u>These inner groups consist of occult students and of those who are in direct or occasional touch with the Masters</u> and of those whose souls are in sufficient control <u>so that the will of the Hierarchy may be communicated and gradually filter down to the channel of the physical brain</u>.[underlined emphasis added]"[36]

Do take note of how, in the third paragraph of the above-cited text concerning the Church, Bailey suggested the use of the Church by "Christ" as "leaven" to "leaven the whole lump" of "seeking souls". This is undeniably a Biblical reference, namely to 1 Corinthians 5:6 and Galatians 5:9. The renowned Bible expositor, Albert Barnes, in his commentary on 1 Corinthians 5:6, explained the symbolism of "leaven" in these verses:

"By <u>leaven</u> the Hebrews metaphorically understood <u>whatever had the power of corrupting</u>, whether doctrine, or example, or anything else. See the note at Matthew 16:6. The sense here is plain. <u>A single sin indulged in, or allowed in the church, would act like leaven - it would pervade and corrupt the whole church, unless it was removed</u>.[underlined emphasis added]"[37]

To those who understand that "leaven" is a metaphor for *sin* and *corruption*, and assuming that Bailey did as well, it is quite plain that her meaning was a nefarious one, proposing that this false Christ is making use of the Church to corrupt the spiritually-receptive members of humanity. It will be demonstrated further that this has been ongoing for centuries. Bailey evidently believed that its *climax* was planned to commence in 2025.

The overall role of Freemasonry in this grand scheme, inasmuch as it has been directed at its highest levels by the militant arm of the self-styled *Universal* Church since just prior to the inception of the American nation, is elucidated in some detail in this author's book, *The Rapture: Fact and Fantasy.*[38] As has been briefly pointed out here, though, the Freemasonic view of one *Great Architect of the Universe* being the object of all faith traditions espouses the same spirit of *that* Church which now actively seeks to unify Christianity with other world religions. As for the role of the education system, this becomes more pointedly obvious than perhaps ever before with the present religiously-oriented legislation.

It can be plainly seen how the passing of the first State law mandating the Ten Commandments in schools in 2025 provides ideological and contextual support for a plan to legislate the national observance of a particular one of those Commandments, in the Project 2025 Presidential Transition Project:

In 2023, a 900-page book was published by the Heritage Foundation entitled *Mandate for Leadership 2025: The Conservative Promise,* subtitled "Project 2025 Presidential Transition Project". The preface explains that the guidance provided in the book is intended to turn the tide of advancing cultural Marxism in U.S. institutions, bring an end to the government behemoth's targeting of American citizens and the conservative values of freedom and liberty, and "return the Republic to its original moorings". It is chiefly concerned with how major federal agencies must be governed. The plan is to put this set of conservative guidelines into practice starting on January 20, 2025, provided that a conservative administration is in place.[39]

This author does not deny, in principle, that these are noble aims worthy of pursuing. However, there is one piece of guidance in the book that does not sit well with those who understand the implications that it carries with respect to Biblical prophecy:

In the eighteenth chapter, "Department of Labor and Related Agencies", under the heading of "Religion", on page 589, is a section entitled "Sabbath Rest" which states the following:

> "God ordained the Sabbath as a day of rest, and until very recently the Judeo-Christian tradition sought to honor that mandate by moral and legal regulation of work on that day. Moreover, a shared day off makes it possible for families and communities to enjoy time off together, rather than as atomized individuals, and provides a healthier cadence of life for everyone. Unfortunately, that communal day of rest has eroded under the pressures of consumerism and secularism, especially for low-income workers.
>
> > **• Congress should encourage communal rest by amending the Fair Labor Standards Act (FLSA)9 to require that workers be paid time and a half for hours worked on the Sabbath.** <u>That day would default to Sunday, except for employers with a sincere religious observance of a Sabbath at a different time</u> (e.g., Friday sundown to Saturday sundown); the obligation would transfer to that period instead. Houses of worship (to the limited extent they may have FLSA-covered employees) and employers legally required to operate around the clock (such as hospitals and first responders) would be exempt, as would workers otherwise exempt from overtime.
> >
> > *Alternative View.* While some conservatives believe that the government should encourage certain religious observance by making it more expensive for employers and consumers to not partake in those observances, other conservatives believe that the government's role is to protect the free exercise of religion by eliminating barriers as opposed to erecting them. Whereas imposing overtime rules on the Sabbath would lead to higher costs and limited access to goods and services and reduce work available on the Sabbath (while also incentivizing some people—through higher wages—to desire to work on the Sabbath), the proper role of government in helping to enable individuals to practice their religion is to reduce barriers to work options and to fruitful employer and employee relations. The result: ample job options that do not require work on the Sabbath so that individuals in roles that sometimes do require Sabbath work are empowered to negotiate directly with their employer to achieve their desired schedule.[underlined emphasis added]"[40]

It can be seen that two opposing strategies for achieving the same objective are given consideration in this section: One proposes the government's encouragement of the religious observance of weekly "Sabbath" rest through negative measures, i.e., by imposing financial penalties on employers who would have employees working on the "Sabbath day", while the other proposes the government's encouragement of that religious observance through positive measures; i.e., by ensuring an abundance of opportunities for employees to work on days other than that day.

Note that both of these recommendations proceed from the notion, as if it were a foregone conclusion, that the government should be proactively "helping to enable individuals to practice their religion", which, in this context, boils down to "helping people to clear out their schedules on (mainly) Sundays so that they will observe them as a day of rest".

The first problem is the underlying presumption that the government has a role in engaging in the promotion of religious practices at all. It is inferred as some unspoken axiom upon which to pivot immediately toward the proposal of legislative measures to that end.

The First Amendment to the U.S. Constitution prohibits the government from making *any law respecting the establishment of religion or prohibiting the free exercise thereof.*[41] It seems that this restriction on government legislation should apply no less in this scenario of making laws to induce the observance of the Fourth Commandment than in that of mandating the display of the Ten Commandments in schools. One has to wonder why the First Amendment is being ignored in both scenarios. Once the government has established precedents by making these laws concerning religion today, what other such laws might they claim to be justified in enacting tomorrow?

The second problem is the designation of the day of the Sabbath in the guidance. Sunday is identified as that day by default, and it is no wonder why, as the vast majority of Christians do traditionally worship on Sundays. However, the Biblical weekly Sabbath is not Sunday but Saturday, the seventh day of the week, according to the Fourth Commandment stated in Exodus 20:10 and Deuteronomy 5:14. If we are to split hairs according to the Jewish tradition of dividing the days, it is from Friday sundown to Saturday sundown.

We do also see in the Project 2025 guidance, at least within the text of the proposed strategy of amending the FLSA to make employers pay overtime for "Sabbath" labor, that exceptions are to be made for employers with a "sincere religious observance of a Sabbath at a different time".

However, one is left to puzzle over just how the *subjective* criterion, "sincere", could be *objectively* qualified in order for such exceptions to be granted for Christians and Judaists who observe the actual Sabbath day. Shall signed, notarized letters from pastors and rabbis and the articles of incorporation of their churches and synagogues be required ? What of those faithful Sabbatarians who are not congregants of any particular church or synagogue? This inherently-flawed premise of anyone's ability to make such a judgement, which is akin to the idea of measuring one's religious belief with a yardstick, seems to be a recipe for unending controversy that will lead to the abandonment of such exceptions, leaving Sunday observance as the only option. Moreover, we find no mention of such exceptions in the text of the "*Alternative*" strategy.

Many will be surprised to learn that this is not the first time that national legislation has been proposed to modify labor laws to enforce the observance of Sunday as a religious day of rest in the United States. On May 21, 1888, Senate Bill S.2983 was introduced by one Mr. M.W. Blair with the stated purpose "To secure to the people the enjoyment of the first day of the week, commonly known as the Lord's day, as a day of rest, and to promote its observance as a day of religious worship". That bill proposed forbidding "secular work, labor, or business to the disturbance of others, works of necessity, and mercy, and humanity excepted", for "any person [to] engage in any play, game, or amusement, or recreation to the disturbance of others on the first day of the week, commonly known as the Lord's day, or during any part thereof, in any Territory, district, vessel, or place subject to the exclusive jurisdiction of the United States", and "for any person or corporation to receive pay for labor or service performed or rendered in violation of this section".[42]

It will be explained further that the repeated efforts to impose a mandatory day of rest in this nation have not been inspired by the pure motives that have been claimed for it. It is neither rooted in the humanitarian desire to give workers a much needed rest from their weekly labors and to allow them assured regular times to spend with their families, nor in the hope of mitigating man-made environmental problems (as has been more recently proposed), nor in a true spirit of piety that wishes to see God honored by the obedience of his faithful people to His Fourth Commandment.

Although these are the cited reasons for such Sunday-rest mandates, which people from diverse walks of life who will support and comply with them sincerely believe, the real reason *is a religious one* —albeit one that could not be further from honoring God than the South is from the North: It is a deception of *Luciferian character*; meaning that it is a ruse of Satan disguised as an angel of light. It is ingeniously devised to fulfill the prophecy of the world's populace worshipping the first beast of Revelation.

The primary blind spot that will prevent most Christians from seeing what is actually happening, and how it is being orchestrated, is a misunderstanding of the timing of the great tribulation and the identity of the antichrist. What will come as a shock to these Christians is the news that this blind spot was put in place *by agents of the antichrist* (carrying out the role of the false prophet of Revelation) through their proliferation of false interpretations of Biblical prophecy intended to obscure his presence and identity. Unfortunately, most will choose to disregard this, and remain oblivious to it, in favor of clinging to their existing beliefs.

"Impossible", they will say, "the man of sin hasn't been revealed yet", or "the antichrist came and went long ago", or "the third temple hasn't been built yet, and what difference does it make, anyway, since *we won't even be here*" or even "the Bible doesn't speak of *the* antichrist; it says that *many* antichrists have come".

If you would like to understand how the Holy Scriptures, along with past history and current events, prove all of the above objections to be misguided, you are invited to continue reading. Once you understand who the antichrist is, all of the rest will fall into place in a way that you could scarcely have imagined.

Otherwise, this author, while hoping the best for you in your continued walk with God and Christ, urges you not to be surprised when you see the pendulum of morality, which *appears* to have swung its limit into the palpable darkness that this nation (and the world) has been immersed in for the last five years and now to be reversing direction—starting its arc back toward *the light,* terminate its current swing at a position not bathed in the warm radiance of God but, rather, in the cold illumination of Lucifer.

"For such are false apostles, deceitful workers, transforming themselves into the apostles of Christ. And no marvel; for Satan himself is transformed into an angel of light. Therefore it is no great thing if his ministers also be transformed as the ministers of righteousness; whose end shall be according to their works."

—2 Corinthians 11:13-15 (KJV)

Prophetic Reeducation 1: The Antichrist is an *Apostate Christian* Entity

One thing that must be understood from Scripture, which is crucially important for us to recognize in these last days but which escapes so many, is that the antichrist was foretold to *arise from within our own Christian ranks*.

When Paul assured the members of the Thessalonian church that Jesus Christ would not return to gather the saints until *after* the occurrence of a great apostasy and the disclosure of the identity of the man of sin (lawlessness)[43], he told them that this person would so exalt himself above every so-called god or object of veneration as to *sit in the temple of God*, exhibiting himself as though he were God:

> "Now we beseech you, brethren, by the coming of our Lord Jesus Christ, and by our gathering together unto him, That ye be not soon shaken in mind, or be troubled, neither by spirit, nor by word, nor by letter as from us, as that the day of Christ is at hand. Let no man deceive you by any means: for that day shall not come, except there come a falling away first, and that man of sin be revealed, the son of perdition; Who opposeth and exalteth himself above all that is called God, or that is worshipped; so that he as God sitteth in the temple of God, shewing himself that he is God."
>
> —2 Thessalonians 2:1-4 (KJV)

In the same message, Paul was clear that this coming man of lawlessness would be the wicked one whom Christ "shall <u>consume with the spirit of his mouth, and shall destroy with the brightness of his coming</u>" (2 Thess. 2:8 KJV). Can there be any reasonable doubt that this entity is the same as the final form of the beast from the sea spoken of in the Book of Revelation who will be thrown into the lake of fire at the Lord's second coming?

> "<u>And the beast was taken, and with him the false prophet</u> that wrought miracles before him, with which he deceived them that had received the mark of the beast, and them that worshipped his image. <u>These both were cast alive into a lake of fire</u> burning with brimstone. And the remnant were <u>slain with the sword of him that sat upon the horse, which sword proceeded out of his mouth</u>: and all the fowls were filled with their flesh."
>
> —Revelation 19:20-21 (KJV)

And, is it not plain enough to understand, from a comparison of Scripture, that this beast of Revelation who "blasphemed against God, his name, and his tabernacle, and those who dwell in heaven" with "a mouth speaking great things and blasphemies" and was permitted to "make war with the saints, and to overcome them" for a period of "forty and two months" (Rev. 13:5-7) is the same entity as the final form of the little horn whom Daniel prophesied would persecute the saints for the equivalent period of time?

> "And <u>he shall speak [great] words against the most High,</u> and <u>shall wear out the saints of the most High,</u> and think to change times and laws: and <u>they shall be given into his hand until a time and times and the dividing of time.</u> But the judgment shall sit, and they shall take away his dominion, to consume and to destroy it unto the end."

> —Daniel 7:25-27 (KJV)

To any who claim that the antichrist rose and fell before the first advent of Christ, namely those who point the finger at the Greek Antiochus IV Epiphanes and can, therefore, only regard John's writings in Revelation concerning the first beast as an account of events that had already happened by his time:

You are hereby challenged to resolve *how that can be true* even as Revelation informs us that this entity would persecute the saints whose patient endurance would manifest in their keeping of "the commandments of God <u>and the faith of Jesus</u>" (Rev. 14:12), as well as *how it can be* that the Apostle, Paul, who lived and wrote 2 Thessalonians 2:1-4 more than two-hundred years after the death of Antiochus,[44] [45] stated that this man of lawlessness would be revealed at some moment *in his future*?

To any who claim that the final antichrist came and went in the first century after Jesus' crucifixion, such as those who identify him as Nero, whose reign ended at his death in 68 A.D.:[46]

You are challenged to carefully consider this: Given that the writing of the First Epistle of John (1 John) is commonly dated at 90 A.D.[47], what sense would there have been in expressing his acknowledgement of the fact that his audience had heard "that [the][48] <u>antichrist shall come</u>" (1 John 2:18), if he believed at that moment that the antichrist had *already* come?

Now, having said the above concerning Antiochus and Nero, one point that this author intends to expound upon in an upcoming book on the prophecy of 2,300 days in Daniel 8 will be briefly summarized here for clarification:

Both the Seleucid Empire, from which Antiochus IV Epiphanes came, and Imperial Rome, from which Nero came, *can* be understood as embodying the little horn *in an imperfect sense*; in that the identity of the little horn was refined over time from a more abstract one to a more concrete one and that both of these empires were integral to that process. The Greek Seleucid Empire can be understood as the cradle from which the nascent little horn *spirit* arose, geographically and philosophically.

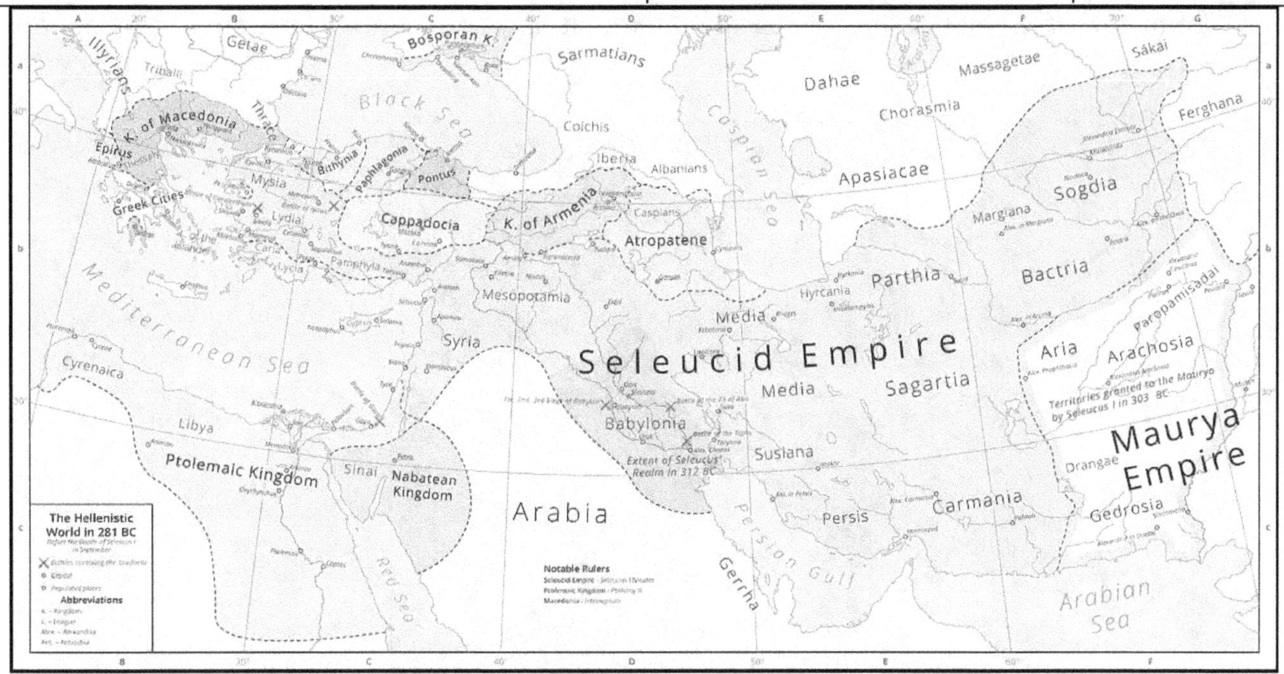

Seleucid Empire ca. 281 B.C. by Cattette. Creative Commons Attribution License[iv]

At the apex of its power, the Seleucid kingdom encompassed the territories of Persia and Babylon as it had waxed great toward the east, the south and the Holy Land, and thus it incorporated the mindsets of those cultures it had consumed with the Greek culture of its conquerors. Note how this amalgamation of Babylon, Persia and Greece seen in the Seleucid Empire mirrors the first three of the four kingdoms symbolized by the sections of the body of the statue in Nebuchadnezzar's dream in Daniel 2 as well as three of the four animalian portions of the body of the beast out of the sea described in Revelation 13:2. The beast has always borne certain traits of mentality inherited from each of these cultures.

However, the final kingdom that completes the persona of the little horn, which is signified by Nebuchadnezzar's statue's legs and feet of iron and by the seven heads, ten horns, and ten crowns of the beast from the sea, is that succeeding, relentless, crushing Roman power which endows it with the stamina to persist until its destruction at the time of Christ's return (Rev. 19:20). This longevity cannot be ascribed to Greece or even *entirely* to *Imperial* Rome.

Pagan Rome can be understood as the *initial* personification of the little horn Power. Daniel 8:9 and 8:21-22 together indicate that a little horn came out of one of the four horns (or kingdoms) into which the initial horn of the Grecian Goat was broken. It is widely agreed that these four horns signify the four main territories into which Alexander the Great's kingdom was subdivided after his death. It is proposed that there is a double meaning in the description of the little horn's "waxing great" in Daniel 8, in that it refers both to the expansion of the initially modest Persian territory into the comparatively massive Seleucid realm as well as the later expansion, and emergence from, within that realm of the little horn personified: Rome.

From the vantage point of God's initial people when they were first conquered by it, Rome did come locally out of the Seleucid territory: Immediately after Rome had, in ca. 64 B.C., annexed the

---

Syrian remnant of the once-vast Seleucid empire, it marched into Palestine and conquered Jerusalem in 63 B.C.

Pompey the Great, the Roman General who led the conquest of Judea ca. 63 B.C.
by Didier Descouens. Creative Commons Attribution License[v]

Although the characteristic little horn spirit of domination and abomination against God's initial and final people can indeed be seen in the actions of the Greek Antiochus through to those of the Roman Nero, it has continued far beyond them in time. It is *only the currently-extant, final personification* of the little horn Power, which arose from among the fragments of Imperial Rome after it was "taken out of the way" (2 Thess. 2:7), who can be identified as the man of lawlessness, the antichrist and the first beast of Revelation.

An engraving of the first beast of Revelation, wearing a three-tiered crown,
from Martin Luther's 1522 German translation of the New Testament

John affirmed that a *singular antichrist* was yet to come, as evidenced by the Greek text analysis below, and then he proceeded to direct the attention of his Christian audience to the fact that the many antichrists who then already existed had emerged *from among their own*:

"Little children, it is the last time: and as ye have heard that [the[49]] antichrist shall come[50], even now are there many antichrists; whereby we know that it is the last time. <u>They went out from us</u>, but they were not of us; for if they had been of us, they would no doubt have continued with us: but they went out, that they might be made manifest that they were not all of us."

—1 John 2:18-19 (KJV)

Moreover. if we take for granted, as we should, that Revelation reveals the truth of the matter that this entity, the first beast, will be destroyed at Christ's *second* coming, then we cannot subscribe to the notion that it has already come *and gone*: The second coming of Christ is not an event that could have occurred in the relatively quiet isolation of a remote region of the Middle East, centuries ago, and since faded from popular memory: We are plainly told that *every eye shall see him* (Rev. 1:7), and it is clear from Scripture that Christ's second coming will *lead to* the destruction of all of his surviving human adversaries along with the beast and the false prophet *and to* the capture and imprisonment of Satan for a period of one-thousand years:

"And I saw an angel come down from heaven, having the key of the bottomless pit and a great chain in his hand. And <u>he laid hold on the dragon, that old serpent, which is the Devil, and Satan, and bound him a thousand years</u>, And cast him into the bottomless pit, and shut him up, and set a seal upon him, that <u>he should deceive the nations no more, till the thousand years should be fulfilled</u>: and after that he must be loosed a little season."

—Revelation 20:1-3 (KJV)

To any who somehow believe that the *present* is that *millennium*, whether in a literal or figurative sense; whether owing to some perceived rationale for re-ordering the chronological sequence of events from how they are presented in the text in Revelation 19-20, so as to view the millennium transpiring *prior to* the return of Christ; or owing to a belief that Christ's second coming already occurred at some point in the distant past in a manner and to an effect completely inconsistent with what is foretold in the Bible, and that the millennium began at that time:

You are challenged to observe how *the agents of evil are still active in the world* and question *how that can possibly be true* if our present era is the extended period of time during which —the language of the above verses constrains us to understand— *Satan's power would be neutralized.* Satan is quite obviously not bound at this time.

The clear commonality between John and his audience that warranted his use of "us" in 1 John 2:18 was that he and they were *all Christians*. He expressed to them that some professing Christians, whom he labeled as "antichrists", had apostatized (i.e., stood away) from the faith. However, a deeper examination of a part of that Greek source text actually reveals more information than meets the eye about the origin of "the antichrist", who, Paul acknowledged, was still to come:

...καὶ **καθὼς** ἠκούσατε ὅτι ὁ ἀντίχριστος ἔρχεται (Greek)
...kai **kathōs** ēkousate hoti antichristos erchetai (Transliteration)
...and **as** ye have heard that antichrist shall come, (King James Bible translation)

καὶ νῦν ἀντίχριστοι πολλοὶ γεγόνασιν... (Greek)[51]
kai nyn antichristoi polloi gegonasin... (Transliteration)
even now are there many antichrists... (King James Bible translation)

When people read this verse in English, they tend, out of habit, to interpret it in the same way as they would a statement like, "As you've heard, the tax auditor is coming next week". In such a sentence, the word, "as", is almost meaningless. In this example sentence, it is a preposition that exists only as a grammatical necessity for introducing the mutually-understood fact of "you've heard". Without the "as" clause, it could simply be phrased as "You've heard that the tax auditor is coming next week" without affecting the core meaning.

What will be shown here, though, is that this tendency causes readers to miss a point of meaning within the original language of this verse that is *profoundly more informative than it seems.*

In this verse, it is the Greek word, "kathōs", that is translated to "as". In modern English, "as" is widely employed for various meanings: it can be a preposition, pronoun, conjunction or adverb.[52]

In the Koine Greek of the New Testament, though, this is not true of the word, kathōs, which is *strictly an adverb.*[53]

Greek Lexicons often supply rich information about the meanings of Greek words and can aid in ascertaining the precise meanings of verses that contain those words in Scripture:

> Strong's Concordance (2531. kathos)
> Usage: **according to the manner in which**, in the degree that, just as, as.

Now, given that kathōs is an adverb in Greek, just *which verb does it refer to* in the clause where it is found? For the sake of clarity, let us base our conclusion on a more literal translation of the Greek that more precisely shows the words of the source text and incorporates the fullest meaning of kathōs given by Strong's:

> ...and/also/namely/even **according to the manner in which** you have heard that the antichrist is coming
>
> and/also/namely/even now antichrists many have come into being...

Can kathōs here possibly describe *the manner in which* John's audience *heard* that the antichrist was coming? Well, it would be nonsensical, at least in this context (and very hard to imagine how it could make sense in any other), to say that *the way* that the *news* about a person's coming *was heard* by the hearer is *the same way* that some *people* have already *come.* It may sound facetious to point out the fact that people cannot travel via sound waves, but that is what a "yes" to this question would suggest. So, we see that the answer can only be "no".

The only other verbal action in the first clause that kathōs can refer to is "is coming", which is grammatically parallel with the verb phrase in the second clause, i.e., "have come into being". Therefore, we are left with the only possible logical meaning of the verse: *The manner in which the singular antichrist is coming*, which *manner*—the verse informs us—John's audience had previously heard about, *was the same manner in which many antichrists had already arisen.* The very next verse then reveals, by the statement, "They went out from us, but they were not of us", that the *manner* referred to is *by way of apostatizing from Christianity.*

With the understanding that the man of lawlessness described by Paul, the little horn of Daniel and the first beast of Revelation all refer to one in the same figure, which is the singular antichrist whom John wrote about, let us now refocus on Paul's phrasing in 2 Thessalonians 2:1-4: "as God sitteth in the temple of God, shewing himself that he is God" and consider it in light of the following New Testament verses that define the temple of God:

> "Now therefore ye are no more strangers and foreigners, but fellowcitizens with the saints, and of the household of God; And are built upon the foundation of the apostles and prophets, Jesus Christ himself being the chief corner stone; <u>In whom all the building fitly framed together groweth unto an holy temple in the Lord: In whom ye also are builded together for an habitation of God</u> through the Spirit."

> —Ephesians 2:19-22 (KJV)

"Know ye not that <u>ye are the temple of God</u>, and that the Spirit of God dwelleth in you? If any man defile the temple of God, him shall God destroy; for the temple of God is holy, which temple ye are."

—1 Corinthians 3:16-17 (KJV)

"And what agreement hath the temple of God with idols? for <u>ye are the temple of the living God</u>; as God hath said, I will dwell in them, and walk in them; and I will be their God, and they shall be my people."

—2 Corinthians 6:16 (KJV)

What is clear from the foregoing analysis of the verses cited in this chapter is that it was foretold that the final, singular antichrist would be a specific *Roman* power that would *apostatize* from Christianity while being *enthroned* in the midst of it, exhibiting itself as being above God, making blasphemous claims, presuming authority to change God's times and laws, and persecuting God's faithful followers.

The greatest obstacle to understanding how the final antichrist can presently exist is the misconception that the period of (great) tribulation is limited to a future handful of years immediately preceding the second coming of Christ. While rightly understanding that this antichrist's persecution of the saints occurs during the tribulation period, those who are misguided in their belief that the tribulation has not yet begun naturally find it impossible to accept that the final antichrist is already here and active. In the next chapter, it will be proven from Scripture and from demonstrating how history already bears witness to a partial fulfillment of end-times prophetic events that this futurist view of the tribulation does not reflect reality.

'Seconda Storia della Notte di San Bartolomeo, 1573' (Second Story of the Night of Saint Bartholomew). Sala Regia - Frescos by Giorgio Vasari and workshop by Sailko[vi]

Prophetic Reeducation 2: The Great Tribulation is *Still Ongoing*

In the interest of publishing this book as urgently as possible before 2025, when the legislation for the Ten Commandments in Louisiana schools is slated to go into force, and probably, as the two events seem to be two prongs of the same strategy, when the next conservative administration will be *installed* and its work to legislate national Sunday rest will commence, the following content of this chapter is borrowed from the relevant chapter of this author's 2023 book, *The Rapture: Fact and Fantasy*.[54]

Illustration of the Whore of Babylon from Martin Luther's 1534 translation of the Bible. Public Domain

"The idea that tribulation will not begin until some moment in the eschatological future is a misconception based on what is apparently willful ignorance of both Scripture and human history.

Take a moment to read carefully one of the many verses in the Bible that is too often glossed over without due attention to what it says:

> *"I John, who also am your brother, and **companion in tribulation**, and in the kingdom and patience of Jesus Christ, was in the isle that is called Patmos, for the word of God, and for the testimony of Jesus Christ"*

—Revelation 1:9

Here, John, writing in the *first century*, begins his letter to the seven Churches by declaring himself to be their fellow *in tribulation*, being imprisoned on Patmos on account of the word of God and the testimony of Jesus.

The word John used was "θλίψει" (thlipsi), tribulation.[55] It is the same word used in Jesus' message to the Church of Smyrna for the tribulation that he acknowledged they had already undergone and would still have to undergo. It is the same word used by the one of the twenty-four elders who told John that the innumerable multitude of the dead he saw standing before the throne of God dressed in white robes were those coming out the great tribulation. It is the same word used by Jesus when he encouraged the disciples in John 16:33:

> *"These things I have spoken unto you, that in me ye might have peace. In the world ye shall have **tribulation**: but be of good cheer; I have overcome the world"*[56]

When Jesus forewarned the disciples (and, by extension, every professing Christian who would read the Bible since then) that they would be delivered unto *affliction*, killed and hated by all nations for his name's sake, Matthew quoted the same word for tribulation, "θλῖψιν" (Matthew 24:9).[57]

Can tribulation be the wrath of God, then? No, quite obviously, it cannot. The wrath of God does not fall on his faithful.

Tribulation is the exercise of the fury of Satan described in Revelation 12:12. It is the persecution of believers on account of their allegiance to God and Christ, the faithful endurance of which equates to spiritual victory over his adversary. Christians throughout history have been persecuted for their beliefs by the Jews, the Romans, other Christians, the Muslims, the Communists and other atheists, to name only some.

Can tribulation, or even *great* tribulation, be confined to just the few years prior to the second coming of Jesus? Let us examine Scripture for the answer.

When Jesus was with the apostles on the Mount of Olives and foretold of the destruction of the temple in Jerusalem that we now know occurred in 70 A.D., he was asked by Peter, James, John and Andrew when that would occur and what the sign preceding it would be. Among the three synoptic gospels, only in Matthew is it recorded that their questions were, rather, what the sign of *his coming* would be and when the *end of the age* (æon) would be. This may reflect that Matthew understood that what they really meant in asking about the temple's destruction —because he shared their mindset— was to inquire when *the end of the world* would be, because they could only imagine that the destruction of the temple could occur at the end of the world.

However, Jesus answered the question in such a way that clarified the destruction of the temple and the end of the world as events that would be separated by time and yet connected by it; that connection being a period of great tribulation that would transpire between them:

When Jesus warned that those in Judaea should flee to the mountains when (as we have already ascertained from Luke 21:20) armies would be seen surrounding Jerusalem, he explained that this would be followed by *great tribulation* such as neither had been, nor ever would be, seen again. He then warned against trusting in false Christs who would come in the mean time before his return. He then spoke of celestial events and anomalies in nature that would be the signs of his coming return, and he said that he would come again *immediately after the tribulation of those days* to gather his elect.

Indeed, the Jews experienced horrific desolation when the Roman armies marched into Jerusalem, both from the attack of the invaders and from fighting amongst themselves, but that was not tribulation for Christians that Jesus had spoken of; that was the wrath of God on that majority of Jews who had rejected their Messiah. Jesus' warning to flee the city was directed to those Jews who would hear and heed it: his Jewish Christian followers.

The point that Jesus was making when he said they should pray that their escape would not occur on a Sabbath was that, if it were, then they would likely be reported by the townspeople, detained and punished for breaking the Pharisaic law against traveling on the Sabbath and so be trapped within the city when the Romans attacked. Thus, he gave an example of how persecution for Jewish Christians would occur in those days, even at the hands of other Jews. Indeed, the first of many general persecutions of Christians began in Rome under Nero in 67 A.D., just three years before the sack of Jerusalem. [58]

The great tribulation is ongoing now and has been for nearly 2,000 years

The key point that tends to be missed is that the great tribulation that Jesus said would occur in *those days* was the *same* tribulation of *those days* that he said he would come immediately *after* (Matthew 24:29; Mark 13:24). As Jesus has not yet returned, *those days* of tribulation have not yet ended. We live in them now.

Although *those days* are now approaching two-thousand years, we must bear in mind that God's perception of the passage of time is unlike ours; therefore his expressions of time in subjective terms like "soon" or "quickly" will not match our mortal sense of urgency. Jesus never said that there would be any cessation, pause, and resumption of the days of great tribulation: On the contrary, Jesus presented the timeframe of great tribulation in such terms that we can understand it as a continuous condition in the world from the time of Nero until his second coming, and, indeed, we can look back and see that history has proven Jesus' forecast to have been correct.

We can plainly see that the persecution of Christians *has* been ongoing for nearly two millennia. It has come in waves of varying levels of severity, more pronounced at different moments in time and more intense in some parts of the world than in others, but it is ever expanding, and by the last days we should expect that it will be worldwide. Can anyone really think that tribulation and the mark of the beast will only ever be faced by those living within a handful of years prior to the return of the Lord?

Jesus' Description of Tribulation in Matthew 24

1 And Jesus went out, and departed from the temple: and his disciples came to *him* for to shew him the buildings of the temple. 2 And Jesus said unto them, See ye not all these things? verily I say unto you, <u>There shall not be left here one stone upon another, that shall not be thrown down.</u>

3 And as he sat upon the mount of Olives, the disciples came unto him privately, saying, Tell us, when shall these things be? and what *shall be* the sign of thy coming, and of the end of the world?

4 And Jesus answered and said unto them, Take heed that no man deceive you.

5 For many shall come in my name, saying, I am Christ; and shall deceive many. 6 And ye shall hear of <u>wars and rumours of wars</u>: see that ye be not troubled: for all *these things* must come to pass, but the end is not yet. 7 For <u>nation shall rise against nation, and kingdom against kingdom: and there shall be famines, and pestilences, and earthquakes</u>, in divers places. 8 All these *are* the beginning of sorrows.

9 Then shall they <u>deliver you up to be afflicted, and shall kill you: and ye shall be hated of all nations for my name's sake.</u> 10 And then shall many be offended, and shall <u>betray one another</u>, and shall <u>hate one another</u>. 11 And many false prophets shall rise, and shall deceive many. 12 And because <u>iniquity shall abound, the love of many shall wax cold</u>. 13 But he that shall endure unto the end, the same shall be saved. 14 And this <u>gospel of the kingdom shall be preached in all the world</u> for a witness unto all nations; and then shall the end come.

15 When ye therefore shall see the <u>abomination of desolation, spoken of by Daniel the prophet, stand in the holy place</u>, (whoso readeth, let him understand:) 16 Then let them which be in Judaea flee into the mountains: 17 Let him which is on the housetop not come down to take any thing out of his house: 18 Neither let him which is in the field return back to take his clothes. 19 And woe unto them that are with child, and to them that give suck in those days! 20 But pray ye that your flight be not in the winter, neither on the sabbath day: 21 For **then shall be great tribulation**, such as was not since the beginning of the world to this time, no, nor ever shall be. 22 And except those days should be shortened, there should no flesh be saved: but for the elect's sake those days shall be shortened. 23 Then if any man shall say unto you, Lo, here *is* Christ, or there; believe *it* not. 24 For there <u>shall arise false Christs, and false prophets</u>, and shall shew great signs and wonders; insomuch that, if *it were* possible, they shall deceive the very elect. 25 Behold, I have told you before.

26 Wherefore if they shall say unto you, Behold, <u>he is in the desert; go not forth</u>: behold, <u>he is in the secret chambers; believe *it* not</u>. 27 For <u>as the lightning cometh out of the east, and shineth even unto the west; so shall also the coming of the Son of man be</u>. 28 For wheresoever the carcase is, there will the eagles be gathered together.

29 Immediately **after the tribulation of those days** shall the sun be darkened, and the moon shall not give her light, and the stars shall fall from heaven, and the powers of the heavens shall be shaken: 30 And <u>**then shall appear the sign of the Son of man in heaven**</u>: and then shall all the tribes of the earth mourn, **and they shall see the Son of man coming in the clouds** of heaven with power and great glory. 31 And <u>he shall send his angels with a great sound of a trumpet, and they shall gather together his elect</u> from the four winds, from one end of heaven to the other.

Jesus' message to every one of the seven Churches in Asia Minor exhorted it to *overcome*: to overcome to eat of the tree of life in the midst of the paradise of God; to overcome to not be hurt by the second death; to overcome to eat of the hidden manna; to overcome to be given power over the nations; to overcome to be clothed in white raiment and to not have their name blotted out from the book of life; to overcome to be made a pillar in the temple of God. Those churches also symbolized the Body of Christ through the ages. What could it mean for them to overcome unless there would be adversity?

In 177 A.D., in the city of Lugdunum in Roman Gaul (now Lyon, France), forty-eight Greek and French-Roman Christians, including a fifteen-year old boy, all for the offense of refusing to renounce Jesus Christ and make sacrifices to the gods of the Romans, after having been banned from appearing in public places lest they be beaten and robbed by the local citizens, were later charged with the crimes of incest and cannibalism (based on false accusations made under duress by two of their pagan servants) and then imprisoned, tortured, and finally thrown to wild animals. [59]

In 516 A.D., in Yemen, Joseph Dhu Nuwas, the Jewish Himyarite king, killed over 22,000 Christians in the cities of Zafar and Najran because they refused to renounce Christ and convert to Judaism, and then he boasted of the achievement.[60]

In 1793, during the dechristianization of France in the midst of the French Revolution, once the citizens of Vendée in Western France had dared to take up arms to fight for the reopening of their churches, the primarily Catholic Christian population of Vendée was targeted in a sustained campaign of massacres of its men, women and children, resulting in a death toll of between 117,000 and 500,000 over a three-year period.[61]

Beginning in 1899, the anti-Christian Boxer Rebellion in China took the lives of 53 children, 136 Protestant missionaries, 47 Catholic priests and nuns, 30,000 Chinese Catholics, 2,000 Chinese Protestants, and between 200 and 400 Russian Orthodox Christians.[62]

During the 20th century, by its collapse in 1991, the government of the Soviet Union had murdered an estimated 500,000 Russian Orthodox Christians for their beliefs, in addition to an unknown number of believers of other denominations.[63]

In his book, *Marx & Satan*, the late Reverend Richard Wurmbrand, who had spent fourteen years over two separate terms in prison in Communist Romania for expressing his Christian beliefs and for preaching the gospel, recounted how the Marxists there mocked and humiliated Christian prisoners by forcing them to take Communion with feces and be "baptized" by having their heads immersed in a bucket of urine. Wurmbrand wrote than an Orthodox Priest he had met inside had had his teeth knocked out with an iron rod in an attempt to make him profane God. The priest reported that the reason his torturers gave for this was, "*If we kill you Christians, you go to heaven. But we don't want you to be crowned martyrs. You should curse God first and then go to hell*".[64]

Presently, in North Korea, it is estimated that over 50,000 Christians, due to their beliefs, are held in concentration camps and regularly tortured, starved, placed in confinement and killed in poison gas chambers as subjects of chemical weapons testing. In that country, Christian faith is a crime under the "anti-reactionary thought" law.[65]

Worldwide, in 2022, according to Open Doors Watch List, a ranking of the fifty countries where Christians face the most extreme persecution, at least 5,621 Christians were killed for their faith, of which 90% were in Nigeria, 4,542 were detained, and 2,110 Churches were attacked.[66]

In Israel, in 2023, a political party called United Torah Judaism proposed legislation that, if passed into law, would make it a criminal offense with a penalty of a one- to two-year prison sentence to preach the Gospel to citizens in the country.[67]

We must realize that our essential perspective as Christians, inasmuch as we are all awaiting the Day of the Lord, is *no different* than that of Christians who have read the same Bible as we have and yet suffered tribulation in times past and, indeed, even now, every day, in places spiritually darker than our free-world minds would care to imagine."[68]

Prophetic Reeducation 3: How and Why You Have Been Deceived

Those who believe that the man of lawlessness has not yet been revealed would do well to look more deeply into the history of the Christian Church—the Great Reformation, in particular—wherein they will discover a truth that is not talked about from most Protestant pulpits today.

"The Antichrist, recognized and declared as such in the confessions of faith of the Protestant Reformers as the Roman Catholic Papacy,[69] maintained its official position as both an ecclesiastical and political authority during the 1,260-year period from 538 until 1798 (the 3½ prophetic years of Daniel 7 and 12 and of Revelation). During that time, it successfully waged war against the true saints of God and overcame them (Revelation 13:7), ultimately having ordered the deaths of tens of millions[70] of accused heretics at the hands of the political authorities that it employed to murder them and break the Sixth Commandment on its behalf."

—*The Rapture: Fact and Fantasy*[71]

The Protestant Reformation, which can generally be said to have taken place between the 1400s and the mid-1700s,[72] exposed the Roman Catholic Papacy as the antichrist, little horn, man of lawlessness and first beast of Revelation, and this conclusion was able to be reached even based on its having only partially fulfilled the characteristics and prophetic events relating to it that are laid out in Scripture.

'Das Zeitalter der Reformation' (The Age of the Reformation) by Gustav Eilers. Public Domain

By the end of the Reformation period, the end of the prophetic 1,260 years—when Scripture indicates the beast of the sea would receive its seemingly deadly wound and, toward the end of which time, the two witnesses would be killed and left lying in the streets—had not yet occurred. However, these events did take place soon enough, during the short span of years comprising the French Revolution and the Dechristianization of France at the end of the 18th century and further galvanized the credibility of the Reformers' accusation.

'Fête de la Raison' (Festival of Reason) in France, 1793. Public Domain

John Wesley, the founder of Methodism, in his *Explanatory Notes on the New Testament* written in 1754, wrote in his commentary on Revelation 13:11 concerning the beast coming up out of the earth, the false prophet, that "he is not yet come, <u>though he cannot be far off. For he is to appear at the end of the forty-two months of the first beast</u>",[73] thus confirming that he acknowledged the active presence of the first beast at his time of writing and believed that its initial 1,260-year reign of tyranny was nearing its end and that this would coincide with the appearance of the second beast.

"We are told that the Two Witnesses would be killed, their bodies left lying in the street while people bid them good riddance and celebrated the affair, but that 3½ days later they would be resurrected. That 3½ days, just as with other time periods in biblical prophecy, should be reckoned on the "year-for-a-day" principle, meaning that this would be 3½ years.

During the program of dechristianization at the time of the French Revolution, for the 3½ years from November 10th, 1793 to June 17th, 1797, the Bible was banned in France. They were gathered up and burned in the streets"[74]

"In 1798, Napoleon of France, Europe's most powerful nation at the time, ordered the invasion of Rome, declared it a Republic and had the then-presiding Pope Pius VI arrested and imprisoned for refusing to relinquish his temporal power, shortly whereafter Pius died. This was the historical fulfillment of the seemingly fatal wound to the head of the first beast mentioned in Revelation 13:3.

It was at just about that time when the second beast began to arise: The United States of America had declared its independence in 1776, been recognized as an independent nation by France by 1778 and ratified its Constitution in 1789. "

—The Rapture: Fact and Fantasy[75]

Not only the Methodists, but Protestants at large staunchly believed that the Roman Catholic Papacy was the antichrist, without any doubt as to its being the same as the man of sin (Lawlessness) and the beast of Revelation who will be destroyed at Christ's coming. So much so that they declared it a fact in their formal confessions of faith, including the notable Westminster Confession, the Smalcald Articles and the Baptist Confession of Faith:

"Chapter XXV OF THE CHURCH.

...

VI.—There is no other head of the church but the Lord Jesus Christ: <u>nor can the Pope of Rome in any sense be head thereof; but is that antichrist, that man of sin, and son of perdition , that exalteth himself in the church against Christ, and all that is called God</u>."

—Westminster Confession of Faith (as of 1881)[76]

"Article IV: Of the Papacy.

...

10] This teaching shows forcefully that <u>the Pope is the very Antichrist, who has exalted himself above, and opposed himself against Christ because he will not permit Christians to be saved without his power</u>, which, nevertheless, is nothing, and is neither ordained nor commanded by God.

11] This is, properly speaking <u>to exalt himself above all that is called God</u> as Paul says, 2 Thess. 2, 4. Even the Turks or the Tartars, great enemies of Christians as they are, do not do this, but they allow whoever wishes to believe in Christ, and take bodily tribute and obedience from Christians."

—The Smalcald Articles[77]

"CHAPTER 26 OF THE CHURCH

Paragraph 4. The Lord Jesus Christ is the Head of the church, in whom, by the appointment of the Father, all power for the calling, institution, order or government of the church, is invested in a supreme and sovereign manner;[7] <u>neither can the Pope of Rome in any sense be head thereof, but is that antichrist, that man of sin, and son of perdition, that exalts himself in the church against Christ, and all that is called God; whom the Lord shall destroy with the brightness of his coming.</u>[8]

7 Col. 1:18; Matt. 28:18-20; Eph. 4:11,12   8 2 Thess. 2:2-9"

—1689 Baptist Confession of Faith[78]

What happened to that belief? Why is this conviction that was once held so strongly now absent from the collective mind, and even the memory, of most of the Protestant populace today?

Observe that these Protestant confessions of faith began to be revised in the late 1800s to remove their statements identifying the Papacy as antichrist. In 1890, the revisers of the Westminster Confession, for example, asserted such justifications for the change as the following:

"We suggest that the Confession contains statements in regard to the Roman Catholic Church which are out of place in a symbol of faith, which can not be sustained by due warrant of Scripture, and ought, therefore, to be omitted."

—Overture on Revision (1890)[79]

"The Westminster divines make an improper use of [2 Thessalonians 2] vers. 3, 4, 8, 9, in order to prove that " the pope of Rome is that Anti-christ, that man of sin and son of perdition, that exalteth himself in the Church against Christ, and all that is called God " (xxv. 6). Here they venture to interpret the apostle's prediction, and apply it to the pope, — a very questionable proceeding in any case, and one not at all becoming in a public Confession of Faith."

—How Shall We Revise the Westminster Confession of Faith? (1890)[80]

Both of these statements gave essentially the same two-fold reason for dismissing the notion that the Roman Catholic Papacy was the antichrist: that such a maligning assertion was inappropriate for inclusion in a statement of faith and that *Scripture itself* was insufficient to *positively identify the Papacy* as this character.

These arguments were weakly contrived. The second was even a kind of "straw-man", as, in reality, the Reformers and those for generations to come after them, including the "Westminster divines", had not based their identification of the antichrist on Scripture *alone*, much less only on verses from a single book and chapter of it (e.g., 2 Thessalonians 2). They had based it on the relevant verses everywhere in Scripture *in combination with the developments in history* that adequately proved their prophetic application to the Papacy.

These revisers' statements seem aligned with the sort of reasoning that would, ultimately, demand nothing less than the identification of the antichrist *by name* in the Bible in order for it to be recognized. Such reasoning would be fallacious, as it is quite obvious that Scripture provides us with the means of identifying the antichrist by revealing the particular characteristics, circumstances and events associated with it. Those identifying aspects can be observed and marked only within the context of unfolding reality as it steadily becomes history. Demanding a precise identification from Scripture itself, which does not provide one as such, would ensure that the antichrist could never be recognized, but such was certainly not God's intention.

Had Scripture supplied *its literal and actual name*, then the antichrist would likely have chosen an alternate one to avoid being easily recognized and to make God seem a liar. Nonetheless, it is still remarkable how closely the meaning of the Papacy's Latin title, *Vicarius Filii Dei*,[81] matches that of the Greek word, *antikristos*: Both terms essentially connote "substitute Christ" from the Christian point of view. It is no surprise that this old Latin title has gradually fallen out of use as the public has become more aware of this linguistic resemblance. As for its *characteristics* and *modus operandi*, though, it is incapable of evading what has been written.

Could the removal of the references to the Papacy as antichrist from these Protestant confessions of faith *really* have been motivated by something else? Might it have been related to the fact that the Roman Church had shown such solidarity with the Protestants on the issue of legislating for a Sunday Sabbath rest only a couple of years prior?

The following is a letter from Roman Catholic Archbishop, James Gibbons, submitted in support of the Sunday Law Bill which was introduced in 1888:

> "   REV. DEAR SIR :
>
> I have to acknowledge your esteemed favor of the 1st instant in reference to the proposed passage of a law by Congress " against Sunday work in the Government's mail and military service," etc.
> I am most happy to add my name to those of the millions of others who are laudably contending against the violation of the Christian Sabbath by unnecessary labor, and who are endeavoring to promote its decent and proper observance by legitimate legislation. As the late Plenary Council of Baltimore has declared, the due observance of the Lord's Day contributes immeasurably to the restriction of vice and immorality and to the promotion of peace, religion, and social order, and can not fail to draw upon the nation the blessing and protection of an overruling Providence. If benevolence to the beasts of burden directed one

day's rest in every week under the old law, surely humanity to man ought to dictate the same measure of rest under the new law.

Your obedient servant in Christ,

JAMES CARD. GIBBONS.
Archbishop of Baltimore. "[82]

As an aside, note the Cardinal's reference to Sunday as "the Christian Sabbath". This is consistent with numerous other mentions of "Sabbath", including within the names of certain organizations, found in the printed public record of the Senate Committee Hearing about the bill, the bill itself mentioned the word "Sabbath" only *once*, in its *concluding two words*, "Sabbath day", whereby it suddenly deviated from its theretofore consistent use of the term, "Lord's Day".[83] It is as though the bill was written in such a way as to avoid referring to Sunday as the Sabbath until absolutely necessary—at its very end, to meet a technical objective of having Sunday enshrined in law as the Sabbath.

As will be noticed in the following excerpt from the record of the Senate Committee Hearing for the Sunday Law bill, the above letter from Cardinal Gibbons was submitted as an unofficial representation of the endorsement of the bill by roughly the entire U.S. population of Roman Catholic citizens at the time. The sheer number of supposed Catholic supporters, theoretically more than seven million people, exceeded even the total number of Protestants represented by the American Sabbath Union that sought for the law to be passed.

"ESTIMATE OF THE PETITIONS FOR A NATIONAL SUNDAY REST LAW.

"Protestants represented in the official membership of the American Sabbath Union, namely: The combined Membership of the Methodist Episcopal Church, the Baptist Church, the Presbyterian Churches, North and South, and the Reformed (Dutch) Church, all of which have officially appointed members of the American Sabbath Union, by whom the law is asked for (practically 6,000,000), 5,977,693; Roman Catholics represented by letter of Cardinal Gibbons appended,* 7,200,000; total 13,177,693.

...

*The letter is not equal in value to the individual signatures of the millions he represents, but no loyal Catholic priest, or paper, or person will oppose what has thus been indorsed."[84]

It will be discussed in the next chapter why the tradition of Sunday observance is so important for the Roman Catholic Papacy to defend and promote, even if doing so means allying itself with Protestants, whom it still regards as heretics[85] [86] but has, for the sake of fostering ecumenical sentiment as long as it suits its aims, conceded to label as "separated brethren".[87] Here, it suffices to inform you that its *claim of authority over Christianity* hinges upon maintaining Sunday worship.[88] [89]

At the zenith of the Reformation period, when that man of lawlessness was being revealed to the world (2 Thess. 2:3), it was the duty of the Jesuit Order, as the sworn defenders of Papal authority, to oppose the spread of that belief. They devised two counterinterpretations of end-times prophecy in order to make it seem impossible in the minds of Protestants for the Papacy to be the antichrist, by projecting the reign of the antichrist into either the distant past or the distant future.

"This was seen in the preterist exposition of biblical end-times prophecy published in 1614 by the Jesuit priest, Luis del Alcázar, which proposed that the Antichrist had already come and gone by the first century,[90] as well as in the futurist exposition made by another Jesuit, Francisco Ribera, in 1590, wherein the reign of the Antichrist was proposed as a distant future event that would not take place until the 3½ years prior to the return of Christ.[91] The Jesuit Ribera's view was the origin of Dispensationalism."

—*The Rapture: Fact and Fantasy*[92]

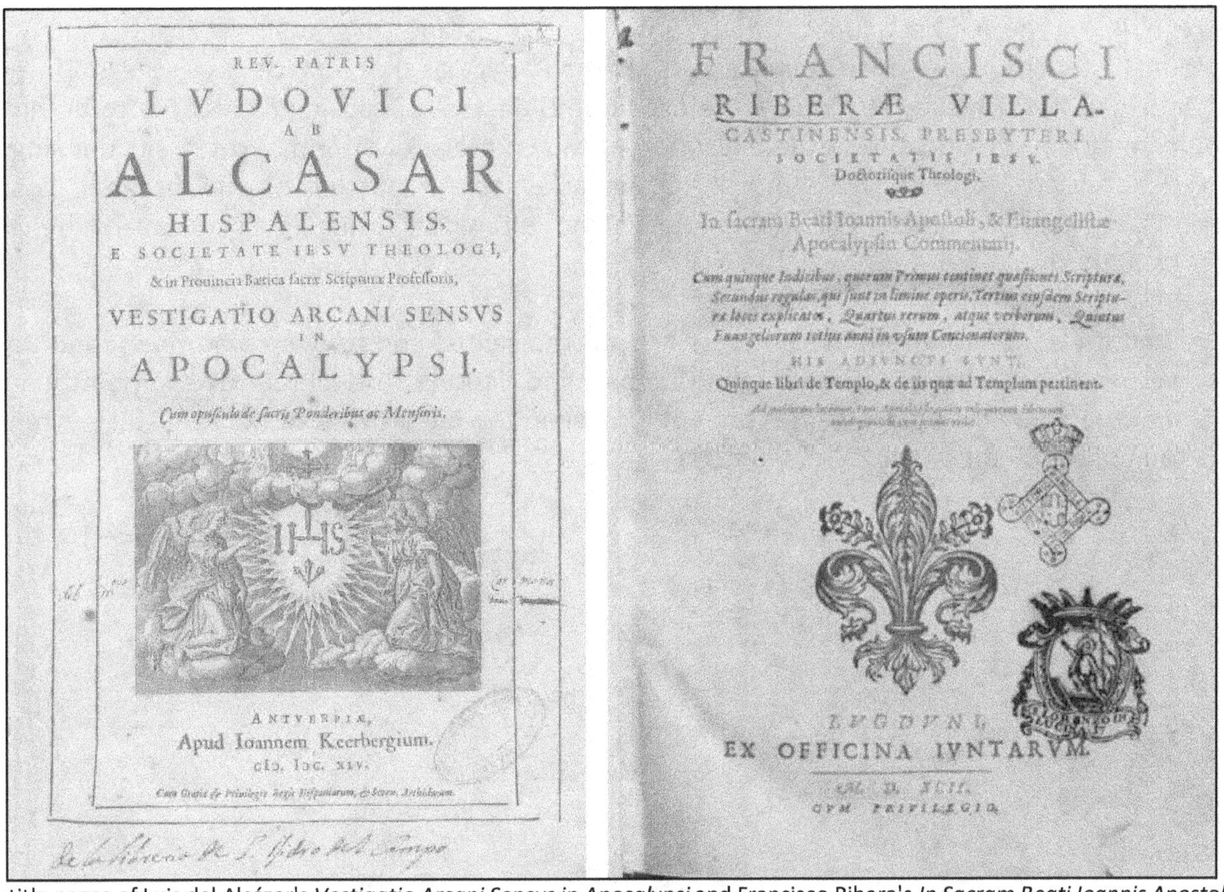

The title pages of Luis del Alcázar's *Vestigatio Arcani Sensvs in Apocalypsi* and Francisco Ribera's *In Sacram Beati Ioannis Apostoli, & Euangelistæ Apocalypsin Commentarij*. Public Domain

Futurism began to increase in popularity within Protestantism during the 1800s. Ribera's original futurist view was furthered during that time by another Jesuit named Manuel La Cunza, who, in 1790, under the pen name of Juan Josafat Ben-Ezra, completed a book entitled "*La venida del Mesías en gloria y majestad*" ("The Coming of the Messiah in Glory and Majesty") which, despite opposition by Roman Catholic authorities (presumably to dispel any notion of a change in *Roman Catholic* eschatology), was circulated in various countries between 1810 and 1826.[93] [94]

Edward Irving, who translated La Cunza's book[95], Samuel Roffey Maitland,[96] John Nelson Darby, and Cyrus Ingerson Scofield were prominent influencers credited with the mid-19th to early-20th-century explosion of Protestant interest in the modified form of futurist eschatology taught in dispensationalism.[97] [98] It is suspected that Jesuit infiltration of Protestant theological seminaries and pulpits[99] has, all the while, exacerbated the spread of the futurist view, which has been to the Papacy's advantage in concealing his identity.

The removal of the warning about the identity of the antichrist from the Protestant confessions of faith coincided rather conspicuously with the alliance of the Roman Catholic Church and American Protestants in advocating for the legislation of a national Sunday day of rest in 1888. This change to doctrine relaxed the preconception of the antichrist in the minds of Protestants enough for them to accept the futurist view, which does not recognize the present existence of the antichrist but, rather, expects (a fictitious) one of non-Christian origin to arise only shortly before the second coming of Jesus.

The resulting surge in the adoption of futurism by Protestants eventually eclipsed that of the prevailing historicist view, which alone recognizes the Papacy as that man of lawlessness. Thus, the final antichrist has achieved its Counter-Reformation objective of causing its identity to be hidden again from all but a relative few. The execution of this strategy of altering Protestant thinking has been a necessary step in the removal of obstacles to its pursuit of the broader goal of reassimilating the "separated" Christian populace and, ultimately, bringing all citizens of the world under its authority.

> "And it was given unto him to make war with the saints, and to overcome them: and power was given him over all kindreds, and tongues, and nations. And all that dwell upon the earth shall worship him, whose names are not written in the book of life of the Lamb slain from the foundation of the world."

> —Revelation 13:7-8 (KJV)

The Meaning of Sunday to the Antichrist

We begin this chapter with selected quotations of statements from Roman Catholic books, periodicals, letters and lectures reflecting their attitudes toward the religious observance of Sunday by Protestants:

"It is worth its while to remember that this [Sunday] observance of the Sabbath, — in which, after all, the only Protestant worship consists, — not only has no foundation in the Bible, but it is in flagrant contradiction with its letter, which commands rest on the Sabbath, which is Saturday. It was the Catholic Church which, by the authority of Jesus Christ, has transferred this rest to the Sunday in remembrance of the resurrection of our Lord. Thus **the observance of Sunday by the Protestants is an homage they pay,** in spite of themselves, **to the authority of the** [Roman Catholic] **Church**.[underlined and bold emphasis added]"

—*Plain Talk about the Protestantism of To-Day*, p. 225[100]

"The [Roman Catholic] Church is above the Bible; and this transference of the observance of Sabbath from Saturday to Sunday is proof positive of that fact. Deny the **authority of the** [Roman Catholic] **Church** and you have no adequate or reasonable explanation or justification for the substitution of Sunday for Saturday in the Third —Protestant Fourth— Commandment of God. [underlined and bold emphasis added]"

—*The Catholic Record*, Sept. 1, 1923, pg. 4, "SABBATH OBSERVANCE" [101]

"Of course the Catholic Church claims that the change [of Saturday to Sunday] was her act. It could not have been otherwise, as none in those days would have dreamed of doing anything in matters spiritual and ecclesiastical and religious without her. And the act is **a mark of her ecclesiastical power and authority** in religious matters. [underlined and bold emphasis added]

(Signed) H. F. Thomas,
Chancellor for the Cardinal
Nov. 11, 1895"[102]

"The [Roman Catholic] Church altered the observance of the Sabbath to the observance of Sunday in commemoration of our Lord having risen from the dead on Easter Sunday, and of the Holy Ghost having descended upon the apostles on Whit Sunday. Protestants who say that they go by the Bible and the Bible only, and that they do not believe anything that is not in the Bible, must be rather puzzled by keeping of Sunday when God distinctly said, "Keep holy the Sabbath Day." The word Sunday does not come anywhere in the Bible, so, without knowing it, **they are obeying the authority of the Catholic Church**. [underlined and bold emphasis added]"

—*The Catechism Simply Explained* (1935 / 1938 Edition)[103] [104]

> "There is <u>but **one church on the face of the earth which has the power, or claims power, to make laws binding on the conscience, binding before God, binding under pain of hell fire. For instance, the institution of Sunday**</u>. What right has any other church to keep this day? You answer by virtue of the third [Protestant fourth] commandment, which says, 'Remember that thou keep holy the Sabbath day.' But <u>Sunday is not the Sabbath</u>. Any school boy knows that Sunday is the first day of the week. I have repeatedly offered one thousand dollars to any one who will prove by the Bible alone that Sunday is the day we are bound to keep, and no one has called for the money. It was <u>the Holy Catholic Church that changed the day of rest from Saturday, the seventh day, to Sunday</u>, the first day of the week. **Which church does the whole civilized world obey**? The Bible says: 'Remember that thou keep holy the Sabbath day,' but the Catholic Church says, 'No, keep the first day of the week,' and **all the world bows down in reverent obedience to the mandates of the Catholic Church**. [underlined and bold emphasis added]"

> —Father T. Enright, President, Redemptorist College, Kansas City, MO
> in a lecture presented in 1884 and apparently also later[105] [106] [107] [108]

Without need of seeing more of many other such statements that could be quoted, it should already be clear enough to the reader that the perspective of the Roman Catholic Church is that it owns the *creator's right* to the tradition of Christian worship on Sundays (which it *boldly* contrasts with *The Creator's claim* to the seventh-day Sabbath, which it confirms is what the Biblical Fourth Commandment actually instructs us to observe) and regards the observance of Sunday worship by Protestants as proof of their submission to its authority rather than that of the Bible.

Now, it will also be briefly observed that there have been attempts by Sunday-keeping Protestant apologists to refute the Roman Catholic Church's claim of having changed the solemnity of Saturday to Sunday, in order to defend the stance that the Protestant practice of Sunday worship is not *pursuant* to Romanist doctrine but is just a tradition held *in common with it* for reasons that are founded on Scripture. The rationale of the typical argument, in a nutshell, is that the Church at the time of the apostles was regarded as the "Catholic Church" but was in no sense the same as the Roman Catholic Church (which refers to itself as, simply, the "Catholic Church") that came into being three centuries later; from which it proceeds to the conclusion that the Roman Catholic Church, not being that genuine, original "Catholic Church" that existed in the apostles' time, cannot rightly claim itself as having been the "Catholic Church" that changed the day because the day was changed by the "Catholic Church" of the apostles![109]

There is no objection here to the assertion that the Roman Catholic Church cannot be regarded as the same Church that existed in the apostles' time or as its successor in the *true spirit* of it. However, despite the claims and even the verified observations of men as to what the Church called itself as time went on, there is nothing *in the Bible* that supports the notion of labeling the primitive apostolic Church as "Catholic", and there is nothing *in the Bible* that evidences the apostles' having *loosed* early Christians from God's Commandment to honor the seventh day or having *bound* them to the observance of any new day of worship.

Frankly, it is astonishing that any Christian would venture to think that the apostles—regardless of the authority that they had been granted by Jesus to manage the affairs of the Church—would ever have dared to countermand their Lord's solemn vow: "For verily I say unto you, **Till heaven and earth pass**, one jot or one tittle shall in no wise pass from the law, till all be fulfilled" (Matthew 5:18).

Gold coin minted in 313 A.D. depicting Constantine the Great with Sol Invictus (a.k.a. Apollo) behind him. Public Domain[vii]

What *there is*—though certainly not in the Bible, but in history—is a series of formal decisions that were made, beginning during the reign of the first "*Holy* Roman Emperor", Constantine, in 321 A.D., progressing to the Synod of Laodicea in 363 A.D.[110] and then on to the Third Council of Orléans[111] in 538 A.D., which, through increasing strictures, displaced the Biblical Sabbath with a Sunday day of rest. Semantic perplexities aside, the greater issue is that the Roman Catholic Church which effectively boasts of having defied the Law of God *is* the Catholic Church that we are dealing with today. Regardless that the abovementioned councils which made those decisions presuming to change the Sabbath day to Sunday were not *exclusively of Roman* Bishops and that the Papacy, *per se*, did not yet exist at those times, the fact that the present Roman Catholic system claims responsibility for those past decisions reveals that it self-identifies with those who did and, thereby, aligns itself with the *spirit* which contests and presumes superiority over the authority of God and Christ.

> "Who opposeth and exalteth himself above all that is called God, or that is worshipped; so that he as God sitteth in the temple of God, shewing himself that he is God"
>
> —2 Thessalonians 2:4 (KJV)

Despite all of the differences in beliefs and practices among Roman Catholicism, Orthodoxy and Protestantism, and the many points of discord that have fragmented Protestantism into its various denominations, there is a single point on which, more than any other, they are all unified: the tradition of Sunday worship. This came about by design.

[vii] https://commons.wikimedia.org/wiki/File:Constantine_multiple_CdM_Beistegui_233.jpg

"God sets forth the Sabbath as the sign or mark of His power and the papacy sets forth the Sunday as the sign or mark of his power. Therefore it is certain that the Sabbath is God's sign or mark and the Sunday institution is the sign or mark of the Papacy. And when the issue is plainly set before the people and they deliberately choose to honor and worship the beast (Papacy) by keeping his institution, and persecute by oppressive laws those who obey God and keep His commandments, the vials of God's wrath will soon be poured out upon the persecutors, and the Lord will come and take His tried and tested people to the mansions He has gone to prepare for them. The conflict is already here. All over the land the cry is raised for more stringent Sunday laws, and soon legislators will yield to the pressure and the mark will be enforced and none but the true hearted will be able to stand."

—*Experiences of a Pioneer Minister of Minnesota* (1892)[112]

Scripture informs us that sin is the transgression of the law (1 John 3:4); literally translated as "lawlessness".[113] The violation of the Fourth of the Ten Commandments, the moral law there referred to, is no less a transgression of the law than that of any of the other nine. It is quite appropriate for the antichrist to be called the "man of lawlessness", given that it entices God's final people—and in fact, the whole world—to rally around it by their unwitting commission of that sin which it portrays as an act of piety.

The *Catechism of the Catholic Church* defines the weekly Sabbath as follows:

"**SABBATH**: The Sabbath or seventh "day," on which God rested after the work of the "six days" of creation was completed, as recounted in the opening narrative of the Bible. Creation is thus ordered to the Sabbath, the day to be kept holy to the praise and worship of God. Just as the seventh day or Sabbath completes the first creation, so the "eighth day," Sunday, the day of the week on which Jesus rose from the dead, is celebrated as the "holy day" by Christians — the day on which the "new creation" began (345 – 349). Thus the Christian observance of Sunday fulfills the commandment to remember and keep holy the Sabbath day (2175)."[114]

Notice carefully how the Catechism, while acknowledging the seventh day Sabbath as "the day to be kept holy to the praise and worship of God", employs the fallacy of equivocation (itself embedded within an incongruous analogy) to advance the notion that, because the Sabbath day *marked the completion* of God's original creation, it somehow follows that Sunday, the day on which Christ was resurrected, *marks the beginning* of the "new creation" that supercedes the original and, therefore, that Sunday replaces the Sabbath day for the purpose of fulfilling the Commandment to honor the Sabbath day.

The fault of equivocation is seen in the premise that the *creation of the heavens and the earth* is a concept that is similar or parallel in nature or character, and therefore validly comparable, to the "new creation" that is referred to. The error of this becomes obvious in light of the understanding that the "new creation" spoken of *in Scripture*, as in 2 Corinthians 5:17, refers to each *reborn individual person* who *has chosen* to be in Christ, not to an all-encompassing reality such as God's creation in Genesis. Apologies if this deconstruction of the single passage in the Catechism has been as mentally taxing to read as it was to write. It is just a small sample of the intricacy of the deception.

This manner of sophistry—making one thing seem to mean another when it does not, and then using that as a launching pad to another conclusion, and so forth—is part and parcel of this doctrine. It draws terms and concepts from Scripture, often blending them with appealing yet misguided human concepts, and then misapplies them in a practical sense to align with its goals. It has no alternative but to resort to such tactics in order to seem to credibly explain and defend ideas that are not actually found in Scripture while still giving them the appearance of being biblically-based.

At this point, a fair question to ask would be how the Protestant catechisms define the day of the Sabbath Commandment by comparison. We will examine a few here:

The Baptist (Keach's) Catechism

"Q. 63. What is required in the fourth commandment ?

The fourth commandment requires the keeping holy to God <u>one whole day in seven</u>, to be a Sabbath to himself.

Q. 64. Which day of the seven hath God appointed to be the weekly Sabbath?

A. Before the resurrection of Christ, God appointed the seventh day of the week to be the weekly Sabbath, and <u>the first day of the week, ever since, to continue to the end of the world, which is the Christian Sabbath</u>."[115]

The Westminster Shorter Catechism

"Q. 58. What is required in the fourth commandment?

The fourth commandment requireth the keeping holy to God such set times as he hath appointed in his word; <u>expressly one whole day in seven</u>, to be a holy Sabbath to himself.

Q. 59. Which day of the seven hath God appointed to us the weekly Sabbath?

From the beginning of the world to the resurrection of Christ, God appointed the seventh day of the week to be the weekly Sabbath; and <u>the first day of the week, ever since, to continue to the end of the world, which is the Christian Sabbath</u>."[116]

The Heidelberg Catechism

"103. What doth God require in the fourth command?

First, that the ministry of the gospel and the schools be maintained (2 Tim. 2 ; 2) ; and that I, especially on the Sabbath, that is, on the day of rest, diligently frequent the Church of God (Heb. 10; 25) ; to hear his word, to use the sacraments, publicly to call upon the Lord (Acts 20 ; 7), and to contribute to the relief of the poor, as becomes a Christian (1 Cor. 16 : 2).

Secondly, that all the days of my life I cease from my evil works, and yield myself to the Lord, to work by his Holy Spirit in me, and thus begin in this life the eternal Sabbath (Heb. 4 ; 9-11).

2 Tim. 2 ; 2. —And the things that thou has heard of me among many witnesses, the same commit thou to faithful men, who shall be able to teach others also. —1 Cor. 9 ; 11, 14. —Deut. 12 : 19.

Heb. 10 ; 25. —Not forsaking the assembling of ourselves together, as the manner of some is : but exhorting one another. —Acts 2 ; 42, 46. —1 Cor. 14 ; 19, 29, 31.

Acts 20 ; 7. —And <u>upon the first day of the week</u>, when the disciples came together to break bread, Paul preached unto them. —Ps. 68 ; 26. —Acts 1 ; 14. —1 Tim. 2 ; 1-3. —Acts 17 ; 2.

1 Cor. 16 ; 2. —<u>Upon the first day of the week</u> let every one of you lay by him in store, as God hath prospered him —Ezek. 20; 12. —Isa. 58; 13, 14.

Heb 4 ; 9-11. —There remaineth therefore a rest to the people of God Let us labor therefore to enter into that rest, lest any man fall after the same example of unbelief. —Isa. 66 ; 23."[117]

Luther's Small Catechism

"47. What is God's object in giving us this commandment ?

That we should set apart <u>one day in seven</u>, as a day of rest, and keep it holy by devoting it to communion with God and divine things.

48. What day was observed in the old dispensation ? The seventh day of the week ; because God rested on the seventh day, and blessed and hallowed it. (Gen. 2:2, 3.)

49. <u>Why do we Christians keep the first day of the week</u> ?

Because on this, " the Lord's day " (Rev. 1 : 10.), the work of redemption was completed by the resurrection of Christ; and his Church was founded by the outpouring of the Holy Ghost. (Mark 16 ; Acts 2.)"[118]

The Protestant Catechisms quoted above reveal a common thread of belief running through them, which is stated outright in most of them: that the language of the Fourth Commandment meant only that *a day in every seven*, rather than *the common seventh day of the week*, should be observed as the Sabbath day. Now, this is a slippery one: On one hand, the Hebrew does use the definite article, i.e.,"*the* seventh day". On the other, it could be said that this makes the seventh day *definite only in contrast* to the "six days you shall work".

The second and more obvious shared point of agreement among them, which may seem paradoxical in light of the first, is that Christians should honor the *first day of the common week*, which is Sunday, rather than the *seventh day of the common week*.

The idea is that all of God's people have honored the Commandment by working for a period of six days and resting on a seventh day, though the seven-day Sabbath cycle period was different for the Israelites than it is for the Christians. In this view, for the Israelites, the seven days of the Sabbath cycle period just happened to correspond to the numbered sequence of the days of the common week, whereas for Christians, the seven-day Sabbath cycle period begins and ends one day later.

Now, see how the second point relies on the first: To assert that the seven-day Sabbath cycle period for Christians begins and ends a day later than it did for the Israelites, based on the claim that this divergence went into effect for Christians at the resurrection of Christ, to avoid any perceived contradiction of God's stipulation of "the *seventh* day" while observing the *first* day of the week, it is necessary for Christians to adopt the stance that the Commandment did not actually refer to the numbered days of the common week.

Immediate difficulty in supporting this position is found in the fact that the Israelites *evidently did understand* "the seventh day" (יוֹם֙ הַשְּׁבִיעִ֔י)[119] *in their own language* as meaning *the seventh day of the common week*, as they did observe that day as the Sabbath. This tends to contradict the claim that the numbered days of the common week were not what were meant by the Commandment.

The fundamental obstacle, though, is that there is no statement anywhere in the Bible indicating that either Yahweh, Jesus or any apostle made Sunday (i.e., the first day of the week) the day of weekly Sabbath observance for Christians.

Moreover, the assertion that *a specific day of the common week did* become the Sabbath day *for Christians* only serves to contradict the premise that the Commandment did not actually refer to the numbered days of the common week!

The following verses, understood in their interconnection, preclude that any part of the moral law will be repealed any time prior to execution of the sentencing of the final judgement. This makes complete sense from a legal perspective, as it would be viewed as unfair and would bring into question the very integrity of God's sense of justice for people who have broken the law to be punished for those deeds (Rev. 20:12-13) *after* that law had been repealed.

> "For verily I say unto you, <u>Till heaven and earth pass</u>, one jot or one tittle shall in no wise pass from the law, till all be **fulfilled** [γένηται, Strong's #1096: **γίνομαι**]"
> —Matthew 5:18 (KJV)

> "And whosoever was not found written in the book of life was cast into the lake of fire. And I saw a new heaven and a new earth: for <u>the first heaven and the first earth were passed away</u>; and there was no more sea"
> —Revelation 20:15-21:1 (KJV)

> "And he said unto me, <u>It is **done**</u> [Γέγοναν, Strong's #1096: **γίνομαι**]. I am Alpha and Omega, the beginning and the end. I will give unto him that is athirst of the fountain of the water of life freely."
> —Revelation 21:6 (KJV)

All finer details aside, it can be seen that Roman Catholics and Protestants (generally), agree that the day was changed to Sunday beginning with the resurrection of Christ. However, let no one be fooled into thinking that the Protestants arrived at this conclusion independently. They passively inherited this belief from the "Mother Church" with which they had long been associated prior to their separation from it. By contrast, history shows that factions of the Christian Church which have *not developed under the influence of Rome* have also *not thought to change the time of the Sabbath law* to Sunday:

> "The Seventh-day Baptists have, from the first, contended that the Sabbath was changed, not by Christ or his Apostles, but by ecclesiastical synods and councils. This could only be proved convincingly by reference to the practice of those churches who were removed by distance or otherwise beyond the pale of such authority. That the Armenian, East Indian, and Abyssinian [Ethiopian] Episcopacies were so removed, and that they absolutely refused to succumb to the authority of the Latin or Greek prelates, sustaining in consequence the most cruel and desolating wars, is an undeniable historical fact ; no less so the truth that during all this time they have been living witnesses against AntiChrist, as the observers of the ancient Sabbath, which practice they learned from the Apostles, or their immediate successors."

> *—A General History of the Sabbatarian Churches* (1851)[120]

The belief in this change of the day, which is without a scriptural foundation, nonetheless unites Protestantism with Roman Catholicism in forsaking the only one of the Ten Commandments that identifies the lawgiver as Yahweh, the Creator of all things through Christ (John 1:3), his Word.

This is the design of the final antichrist, through whom the Adversary seeks to usurp the authority of God and receive the obedience that is due to Him through the Fourth Commandment by altering its time, significance and manner of observance.

The spirit of antichrist is associated in Scripture with Apollo the Destroyer (i.e. the Greek "Apollyon"[121] and Hebrew "Abaddon" named in Rev. 9:11; 17:8), who is also known in Greco-Roman tradition by the names of Helios and Sol Invictus. This is the same Sun god in whose honor Holy Roman Emperor Constantine dedicated "the Venerable Day of the Sun" as a day of weekly rest in the Roman Empire in 321 A.D.[122] Apollo is recognized in mythology as being the son of Zeus-Jupiter, whom Christ indirectly identified as Satan to those who understand the reference to the "throne of Satan" in Pergamon (i.e., the Pergamon Altar) in Revelation 2:13.

This antichrist spirit has, for centuries, been at work redirecting the Christian practice of Sabbath worship to the Day of the Sun in his own honor. Satan knows that Sun worship has always been viewed by God as one of the greatest of men's abominations (Ezekiel 8:15-18), and he adopts the symbol of the Sun both to signify his Luciferian name, הֵילֵל, (Hê·lêl, "Shining One"; cf. Isaiah 14:12) and to taunt God.

It is also relevant that the goddess, Diana, or Artemis, Apollo's sister, symbolized by the Moon, represents the feminine form of the masculine Sun god.[123] Note that Artemis was regarded in pagan Rome as a perpetual virgin.[124] This solar-lunar dualism of the very same deity under different names is seen in the pairing of Baal and his wife, the goddess Ashtoreth (also known as Astarte,[125] called Ishtar by the Babylonians[126] and Isis by the Egyptians[127]), who is mentioned in the Old Testament (1 Kings 11:5). Worshipped through the Moon as the "Queen of Heaven"[128] (as seen within Jeremiah 7 and 44), this title is used in Roman Catholicism to refer to its rendition of the Virgin Mary.[129]

In Roman Catholicism, the monstrance, or ostensorium, which is the vessel used in its Eucharist ritual for displaying the consecrated host (i.e., the communion wafer after its having been (supposedly) transformed into the literal body of Christ), is typically of an overall sunburst design. The component in the center of the monstrance upon which the disc-shaped wafer is placed, called the lunula, or lunette, is very often shaped like a crescent moon. By the way, the same figure of the Sun (often rendered simply as a star, disc or cross) embraced by the crescent Moon is found in ancient depictions of Egyptian deities, in the symbol of Islam, and even subtly disguised within the hammer & sickle emblem of supposedly atheistic communism. It is a common *trademark*, as it were, signifying various forms of expression of the Mystery of Iniquity (2 Thess. 2:7).

Catholic Monstrance[a], Islamic seal[b] and Soviet Communist flag[c]. Creative Commons Attribution Licenses / Public Domain[viii]

The Sun and Moon symbology in Romanism is also seen as reflective of the embodiment of ecclesiastical *and* temporal powers by the Church and the superiority of the former to the latter:

> "the sun and the moon are placed in the firmament, the greater as the light of the day, and the lesser of the night ; thus are these two powers in the church ; the pontifical, which, as having the charge of souls, is the greater, and the royal, which is less, and to which the bodies of men only are trusted."

—Pope Innocent III[130]

At every Sunday Mass in hundreds of thousands of parishes around the globe, this spirit of the solar-lunar duality is expressed in the Roman Catholic sacrament of the Eucharist. At the core of each one is a *newly*-crucified Jesus Christ. As Pope Francis has said, "...the day of rest [*Sunday*], *centred on the Eucharist, sheds its light* on the whole week..." [italicized emphasis added].[131] What light is shed by Sunday—that of God or of the Shining One?

Those who see Christ's resurrection on Sunday as an act of His *sanctification* of that day are deceived to the extreme: His resurrection on Sunday was a symbolic act of His *defiance* against the adversary, who identifies itself with, and seeks to achieve its aims by encouraging worship on, that day. This is the same defiance that Christ showed when he declared that he would build his Church "over[132] this rock", when he and his disciples stood in Cæsaria Philippi at the foot of *Mount Hermon*[133] (Matthew 16:13-18), *the tallest "rock" in Syria*,[134] onto which two-hundred fallen angels are reputed to have descended[135] centuries before and commenced their Satanic composite plan of obstructing the Israelites' settlement of the promised land by populating it with their warlike giant offspring and—failing that—of corrupting the bloodline of the Messiah with their seed before he would be born.

Read the terms of the Fourth Commandment given in Exodus 20:8-11 and then compare closely with it the language in the verses of Revelation quoted below it:

"Remember the sabbath day, to keep it holy. Six days shalt thou labour, and do all thy work: But the seventh day is the sabbath of the LORD thy God: in it thou shalt <u>not do any work</u>, thou, nor thy son, nor thy daughter, thy manservant, nor thy maidservant, nor thy cattle, nor thy stranger that is within thy gates: For in six days **the LORD made heaven and earth, the sea**, and all that in them is, and **rested** the seventh day: wherefore the LORD blessed the sabbath day, and hallowed it."

"And I saw another angel fly in the midst of heaven, having the everlasting gospel to preach unto them that dwell on the earth, and to every nation, and kindred, and tongue, and people, Saying with a loud voice, Fear God, and give glory to him; for the hour of his judgment is come: and <u>worship **him that made heaven, and earth, and the sea**</u>, and the fountains of waters."

—Revelation 14:6-7 (KJV)

"And the smoke of their torment ascendeth up for ever and ever: and **they have no rest** <u>day nor night, who worship the beast and his image, and</u> [or "namely/even"[136]] **whosoever receiveth the mark** of his name. Here is <u>the patience of the saints</u>: here are <u>they that keep the commandments of God</u>, and the faith of Jesus."

—Revelation 14:11-12 (KJV)

After all that has been explained here, one should be able to discern within these verses in Revelation very strong clues indicating that the worship of the beast and his image, and its mark, will be related to the issue of obedience to the Fourth Commandment.

This author urges you to consider *how peculiar it seems* for Scripture to say a thing like "they have no rest" in describing those who will have received the mark of the beast unless its meaning is inferred from another scriptural reference. Moreover, the next verse in the passage makes it clear that the resistance given by the faithful believers to the worship and the mark of the beast will involve their *keeping of God's Commandments*. Do you recognize the references to the Fourth Commandment? The signs are given for the benefit of those who are willing to see them.

Pope Francis, in his 2015 encyclical letter, *Laudato Si: On Care for Our Common Home*, advocating environmental stewardship and the recognition of the interconnectedness between God, humans, and the Earth, saw fit to extol the benefits of *rest on Sunday*, likening it to the "Jewish" Sabbath and characterizing it as a motivator of increased common *concern for nature* and the poor:

"237. On Sunday, our participation in the Eucharist has special importance. <u>Sunday, like the Jewish Sabbath</u>, is meant to be a day which heals our relationships, with God, with ourselves, with others and with the world. Sunday is the day of the Resurrection, the "first day" of the new creation, whose first fruits are the Lord's risen humanity, the pledge of the final transfiguration of all created reality. It also proclaims "man's eternal rest in God".[168] In this way, Christian spirituality incorporates the value of relaxation and festivity. We tend to demean contemplative rest as something unproductive and unnecessary, but this is to do away with the very thing which is most important about work: its meaning. We are called to include in our work a dimension of receptivity and gratuity, which is quite different from mere inactivity. Rather, it is another way of working, which forms part of our very essence. It protects human action from becoming empty activism; it also prevents that unfettered greed and sense of isolation which make us seek personal gain to the detriment of all else. <u>The law of weekly rest forbade work on the seventh day</u>, "so that your ox and your donkey may have rest, and the son of your maidservant, and the stranger, may be refreshed" (Ex 23:12). Rest opens our eyes to the larger picture and gives us renewed sensitivity to the rights of others. <u>And so the day of rest, centred on the Eucharist</u>, sheds its light on the whole week, and <u>motivates us to greater concern for nature and the poor</u>. [underlined emphasis added]

[Footnote: [168] *Catechism of the Catholic Church*, 2175.]"[137]

Characterizing the observance of Sunday rest as an act of environmental responsibility is the Papacy's modern strategy for bringing the population of the entire world into obedience to it, in much the same way that its equating vaccination to "an act of love" was meant to guilt Christians into submitting to draconian mandates, for the so-called *common good*, resulting in their acceptance of something which—it has since been exposed—was not at all the safe and effective solution it was claimed to be and which led to the destruction of many.

In the wake of decades of climate-alarmist propaganda, many Christians, followers of other religions, and atheists alike are now conditioned to do whatever is asked of them to stave off the environmental disaster that they have been led to believe is coming around the bend. To park the cars and shut down the factories in order to give Mother Earth a periodic break, a weekly day of rest is proposed. By no mere coincidence, that day happens to be Sunday.

"And he causeth all, both small and great, rich and poor, free and bond, to receive a mark in their right hand, or in their foreheads"

—Revelation 13:16 (KJV)

It will not matter whether the acceptance of the mark, which means obedience to the antichrist's law as opposed to God's law, is motivated by one's belief—represented by the forehead, or merely confirmed by one's actions—represented by the right hand. Either will suffice for Satan. Therefore, the *professed* religion of anyone who accepts the mark, even if that be none at all, will make no difference. The true test of loyalty to God in the coming ordeal will be whether one keeps His Commandments *and* the faith of Jesus (Rev. 14:12). Scripture makes it clear that the former is a reflection of the latter:

"By this we know that we love the children of God: when we love God and keep His commandments . For this is the love of God, that we keep His commandments"

—1 John 5:2 (KJV)

"If you love Me, you will keep My commandments"

—John 14:15 (KJV)

A Warning About the Current Dialectic Shift

In the 2022/2023[138] book, *The Satanic Aim of the United Nations, World Economic Forum & Great Reset*,[139] this author characterized the wave of chaos and evil spreading across America and the world in recent years as "a strategy of demoralization of society—a planned process of devolution meant to manifest a sort of hell on earth—as part of a broader objective of ideological subversion", pointing out the following:

"To be sure, as so many world leaders have aligned their policies with the aims of the WEF and the UN, under the slogan of the "Great Reset" (a.k.a. "Build Back Better"), the general public is being shocked by their blatant encouragement of ideas contrary to traditional concepts of morality and religion, such as...

•education of schoolchildren in transgenderism;[100]

•promotion of socially-divisive movements grounded in Marxist class-struggle ideology, such as Critical Race Theory[101] and the victimology of "Wokeness";[102]

•endorsement of lawlessness and societal decay by decriminalizing crimes like burglary[103] and illicit drug use[104] and handicapping law enforcement in high-crime locales by defunding[105] and imposing vaccination mandates on police departments;[106][107]

•financially incentivizing rather than remedying joblessness and vagrancy;[108][109][110]

•suspending the property rights of property owners and landowners while encouraging delinquency, trespassing, and squatting;[111][112][113][114]

•cutting off critical transnational fuel supply lines;[115][116][117]

•welcoming and covertly resettling hundreds of thousands of unvetted illegal immigrants into society[118][119] while trying to block legislation requiring that citizens properly identify themselves when voting;[120][121][122]

•declaring unconstitutional vaccination mandates on large employers[123] and even the populations of entire countries;[124][125]

•subjecting citizens to extended lockdowns and travel restrictions;[126][127][128]

•censoring any views contradicting their expressed narratives as "misinformation";[129][130]

•denying citizens' rights of assembly and freedom of expression by disrupting legal, peaceful public protests;[131][132][133]

•arming an infamous terrorist group in the Middle East with tens of billions of dollars' worth of advanced military weapons and vehicles[134] while abandoning a substantial number of free-world citizens and their supporters behind that enemy's lines to be hunted down and made examples of.[135] [136]"

•subjecting citizens to extended lockdowns and travel restrictions;[126] [127] [128]

•censoring any views contradicting their expressed narratives as "misinformation";[129] [130]

•denying citizens' rights of assembly and freedom of expression by disrupting legal, peaceful public protests;[131] [132] [133]

•arming an infamous terrorist group in the Middle East with tens of billions of dollars' worth of advanced military weapons and vehicles[134] while abandoning a substantial number of free-world citizens and their supporters behind that enemy's lines to be hunted down and made examples of.[135] [136]"

This "hell on earth" scenario has been a *dialectic* strategy designed to modify the ideology and behavior of already morally-minded people by pushing them to the extreme end of that spectrum. More simply stated, this recent extraordinary dose of wickedness and depravity was intended to be so repulsive to average citizens as to drive them to the brink of their tolerance, so that they would embrace the opposing ideals of right-wing conservativism and "Judeo-Christian values" more zealously than ever before.

Most Christians will probably wonder how that could possibly be seen as a bad thing. Obviously, it sounds like a change for the better, and that is exactly the impression that it is intended to give; however, the real objective of this moral shift is not what it appears to be.

The voice of today's American Christian exclaims, "We have had enough of this ungodliness, the rampant crime in the streets, the acts of arson and shooting sprees in our churches, the blatant promotion of Satanic principles to our children in the public schools, and the Marxist authoritarianism that is trying to take away our God-given liberties including our right to private property and to worship according to our conscience. Our country is turning into a new Sodom, taking good for evil and evil for good. It's about time to do something to turn back the tide before it's too late!".

So, what is to be done?

Well, the Christian Nationalists tell us that the solution is for the nation to turn back to God. To *make America great again*, as they say, Christian morality must be imposed upon the government, which must be held to account for making laws that promote those values. Of course, this means that the Church must be allowed to dictate to the State what is right and good. These are the same Christians who applaud the issuance of the *God Bless the U.S.A. Bible*, which combines Church and State documents,[140] understanding full well what that portends for the country.

The movement of Christian Nationalism is also supported by many well-meaning Protestants and Catholics who do not understand its true objectives and think that moral order should be restored by forcing the government to operate under Christian principles. It is actually designed to reunify Church and State, as a necessary condition for the Papacy to take power again in the position of universal religious leader. To anyone who thinks that this direction leads to the protection of religious liberty for Christians, let it be known that the Roman Catholic system has zero tolerance for the "error" of individual liberty of conscience.

"13. Now We consider another abundant source of the evils with which the Church is afflicted at present: indifferentism. [...] Therefore 'without a doubt, they will perish forever, unless they hold the Catholic faith whole and inviolate.'[18] [...] A schismatic flatters himself falsely if he asserts that he, too, has been washed in the waters of regeneration. [...] 14. This shameful font of indifferentism gives rise to that absurd and erroneous proposition which claims that liberty of conscience must be maintained for everyone. It spreads ruin in sacred and civil affairs, though some repeat over and over again with the greatest impudence that some advantage accrues to religion from it."

—Pope Gregory XVI,
Mirari Vos: *On Liberalism and Religious Indifferentism* (1832)[141]

"Actually We learned from reports and documents just received that a number of men of various sects met in the city of New York last year on June 12 and founded a new society called Christian League. Their common purpose is to spread religious liberty, or rather an insane desire for indifference concerning religion, among Romans and Italians. [...] Therefore they are determined to give everyone the gift of liberty of conscience, or rather of error; they liken it to a fountain from which political liberty and increased public prosperity may spring forth. [underlined emphasis added]"

—Pope Gregory XVI,
Inter Praecipuas: *On Biblical Societies* (1844)[142]

To those who object to the notion of unifying Church and State, on the grounds of the Establishment Clause[143] of the First Amendment to the Constitution, Christian Nationalists within the government give such retorts as:

"The church is supposed to direct the government. The government is not meant to direct the church. That is not how our founding fathers intended it.

"And I'm tired of this separation of church and state junk, that's not in the Constitution. It was in a stinking letter and it means nothing like what they say it does."

—Lauren Boebert, Member of the U.S. House of Representatives[144]

The above statement is only *technically* correct insofar as *the literal phrase* "separation of church and state" is not in the Constitution. This may seem good enough to be sown as the seed of a new urban myth in the fertile imaginations of many who have not read the First Amendment that *the principle* of that separation is not enshrined in the Constitution either, but it does not change the fact that it is.

As for the above assertion that the correct understanding of the intent of the Establishment Clause is that the Church is supposed to direct the government and not the other way around: This is confirmed as a complete falsehood; firstly, by the fact that the Clause makes no mention of the Church directing the government at all, whereas it clearly prohibits the government from making laws concerning the establishment of religion and its free exercise; secondly, by common sense, which makes it plain that even the *Church's directing of the government's making of laws* concerning religion would still mean the *government's making* of laws concerning religion; and, thirdly, by the "stinking" letter written by Thomas Jefferson to members of the Danbury Baptist association of Connecticut on January 1, 1802 to clarify his position on the matter, in which he wrote:

> "Believing with you that religion is a matter which lies solely between man & his god, that he owes account to none other for his faith or his worship, that the legitimate powers of government reach actions only and not opinions, I contemplate with sovereign reverence that act of the whole American people which declared that their legislature should "make no law respecting an establishment of religion, or prohibiting the free exercise thereof;" thus building a wall of [eternal] separation between Church & State."[145]

As an aside, do note that Jefferson, according to document analysts at the FBI, originally wrote "eternal wall of separation" and then omitted the word "eternal".[146] Although this does not detract from the clarity of his sentiment that Church and State were meant to be divided, it may hint that he knew that this separation would not last indefinitely. After all, he was operating among Freemasons.

The American nation was founded largely by Freemasons, who were overseen by Jesuits, as a temporary repository for the controlled management of the unstoppable exodus of Bible-based Christians fleeing from the religious intolerance and persecution of spiritual *Babylon* after the Protestant Reformation began. It was the ultimate manifestation of the "two wings of the eagle" upon which, and the "wilderness" to which, those of the true Church flew to escape "from the face of the serpent". However, they were nourished there only for "a time, and times, and half a time" before it is written that "the serpent cast out of his mouth water as a flood after the woman" (Rev. 12:14-15). This may be understood as meaning the period of time until the United States was formally established, at which point the Jesuit flood began.

The Papacy has, since then, worked to steer American Protestants slowly back toward itself, through its ecumenical gestures and a pervasive end-times doctrine that has almost entirely obscured its identity as the antichrist. The expectation is that these Protestants, weakened in their convictions, having forgotten the lessons of their forefathers, will finally accept the Papacy as the global leader for the theocratic new world order that it intends to establish. Notice how even the use of the term "Protestant" seems to have faded from popular use out of preference for the less-controversial term "Evangelical": no longer protesting; just spreading the message. Is the message of the Gospel silent on the matter of the antichrist?

The false prophet, which—precisely speaking—is the Jesuit Order, most prominently revealed its role as the imager to the first beast at about the time when the latter incurred its deadly wound; that is, at the unveiling of its masterwork, the United States, which is the second beast. The nation has been its primary staging ground for carrying out the objective of causing the people to make an image to the first beast that will cause all who are not saved to worship that image (Rev. 13:15). This image reflects the unification of the Church and State. It was just such a union between the Pharisees and the Romans that led to the crucifixion of Christ. It was also what made possible the murder of tens of millions of Bible-based Christians[147] [148] during the Papacy's initial 1,260-year reign in the Dark Ages (Rev. 13:5-7).

We can see strong hints of this image, or likeness, in the telltale symbols of the ancient Roman little horn power in the United States: its capitol building, a veritable mirror image of the Basilica in Rome; the markedly Roman architecture of government buildings in Washington D.C.; the eagle symbol associated with Jupiter, worshipped in ancient Rome and adopted as its totem. Moreover, we can see it in the Statue of Liberty: that strange composite of the Sun god, Apollo/Sol/Helios, and his feminine alter ego, the Moon goddess, Artemis/Diana, the perpetual virgin, holding the torch of illumination (i.e., of Lucifer) in its right hand and in its left a votive tablet dedicating the birthdate of the nation to that deity.

We also see the image taking shape spiritually as Christians in the U.S. seek to mirror the paradigm of the old Papal theocracy over the European kingdoms in a misguided effort to restore moral order to a world gone insane with evil.

The current presidential administration's allowing of an unbridled influx of illegal immigrants into the United States from Latin America, whose cultures are generally predisposed toward Roman Catholicism, is for the purpose of rebalancing the religious demographic of the population into one that is more inclined toward allegiance to the Papacy.

Samuel Morse, in 1835, expressed his concerns about a threat to the free institutions of the Republic posed by the invasive immigration of Roman Catholics of the uneducated class from Europe occurring at that time:

"Another weak point in our system is our laws *encouraging immigration*, and affording facilities to *naturalization.** In the early state of the country liberality in these points was thought to be of advantage, as it promoted the cultivation of our wild lands, but the dangers which now threaten our free institutions from this source more than balance all advantages of this character. The great body of emigrants to this country are the hard-working mentally neglected poor of Catholic countries in Europe, who have left a land where they were enslaved, for one of freedom. However well disposed they may be to the country which protects them, and adopts them as citizens, they are not fitted to act with judgment in the political affairs of their new country, like native citizens educated from their infancy in the principles and habits of our institutions. Most of them are too ignorant to act at all for themselves, and expect to be guided wholly by others. These others are of course their priests. Priests have ruled them at home by *divine right* ; their ignorant minds cannot ordinarily be emancipated from their habitual subjection, they will not learn nor appreciate their exemption from any such usurpation of priestly power in this country, and they are implicitly at the beck of their spiritual guides. They live surrounded by freedom, yet liberty of conscience, right of private judgment, whether in religion or politics, are as effectually excluded by the priests, as if the code of Austria already ruled the land. They form a body of men whose habits of *action*, (for I cannot say *thought*,} are opposed to the principles of our free institutions, for they are not accessible to the reasonings of the press, they cannot and do not think for themselves.

Every unlettered Catholic emigrant, therefore, that comes into the country, is adding to a mass of ignorance which it will be difficult to reach by any liberal instruction, and however honest, (and I have no doubt most of them are so,) yet from the nature of things they are but obedient instruments in the hands of their more knowing leaders to accomplish the designs of their foreign masters. Republican education, were it allowed freely to come in contact with their minds, would doubtless soon furnish a remedy for an evil for which, in the existing state of things, we have no cure. It is but to continue for a few years the sort of immigration that is now daily pouring in its thousands from Europe, and our institutions, for aught that I can see, are at the mercy of a body of foreigners, officered by foreigners, and held completely under the control of a foreign power. We may then have reason to say, that we are the dupes of our own hospitality ; we have sheltered in our well provided house a needy body of strangers, who, well filled with our cheer, are encouraged by the unaccustomed familiarity with which they are treated, first to upset the regulations of the houshold, and then to turn their host and his family out of doors."

—*Foreign Conspiracy Against the Liberties of the United States: The Numbers of Brutus*[149]

In Europe, the analogous situation today involves immigrants mainly from Islamic countries. However, this author suspects that a bond of Islam to the Papacy will eventually be forged, somehow, likely on the common ground of their shared reverence for Mary.

As perceived improvements within society result from the initial movements in this moral-religious direction, and this ideology thus expands globally, a universal leader will ultimately be sought to head it. There will be only one which the world will acknowledge as qualified: one which will have established congenial relationships with all of the world's religions and which has, all along, esteemed itself as the supreme authority over religious and political matters on earth.

Ample evidence of the truth of that last statement is adduced in the following excerpt from *The Protestant: Essays on the Principal Points of Controversy between the Church of Rome and the Reformed*, which contains quotations of numerous such claims made by Roman Catholic authorities over the centuries:

"I. POPERY AND JESUITISM,

INCOMPATIBLE WITH CIVIL AND RELIGIOUS LIBERTY.

To understand the consequences of popery in society, and the artifices and the acts of the Jesuits, who are the most resolute and devoted servants of the Roman court, we must become correctly acquainted with the principles of the papal system.

The influence of popery upon the civil institutions of the American confederated republics, has not hitherto been urged upon the public attention ; and the idea, that the Italian pontiff can ever attain any control over this country, during its present organization, is openly and generally ridiculed. It is indispensable, therefore, to unfold the claims of the Roman tyrant, respecting his usurped jurisdiction over all the nations of the earth ; and to describe the measures which his chief servants, the Jesuits, are always prepared to adopt and execute, that the authority and exactions of the papal despotism may be extended and prolonged.

Popery claims to be infallible ; and of course it is every where and always the same. The enactments, bulls, canons, and decretals of all former ages, in the estimation of the pontificate, are equally obligatory now, as during the undisputed predominance of " the Man of Sin." It may neither be expedient to assert their validity, nor practicable to enforce them; but though partially dormant among Protestants, they are always ready to be adduced, as the exigencies of the times may permit. There is not a single heresy retracted ; not one outrageous usurpation denounced ; and not even a persecuting canon, decretal, or bull, nullified. The whole mass of direful pretended legislation remains, in all its assumed supremacy ; and is partially reissued, as of permanent and universal force, whenever a favourable opportunity is presented to attack the thoughtless, or to intimidate the ignorant.

To popery and its unholy dogmas, in their spiritual application, this discussion will not advert. The dangerous influence which the extension of Romanism by Jesuitical agents may have upon our country is our topic ; and the following principles, which are held by all Papists as infallibly supreme, will elucidate the interesting inquiry, whether Jesuitism can safely be tolerated in the United States?

'*The supremacy of the pope,*' says Bellarmine, '*is the main substance of Christianity*' —it is therefore indispensable, accurately to know the character of this principal ingredient of the pontifical government. This fundamental doctrine is thus stated by themselves.

Polus, Card, de Concil. page 91. 'Petri cathedram super omnia, &c. Christ hath constituted the chair of Peter, above all imperial thrones, and all royal tribunals.'

Blasius, de Rom. Eccles. Dignitat. Tract. 7. pages 34, 83, 85. 'Unicus Dei Vicarius Pontifex Romanus, &c. The pope's empire is over all the world, *Pagan and Christian*; and he is the only vicar of God, who has supreme power and empire over all kings and princes of the earth. As there is one God, the Monarch of all, who presides and rules over all mortals, so there is one vicar of God. Kings ought to be under Peter, and must bow down and submit their necks to him and his successors ; who is Prince and Lord of all, whom all emperors, kings, and potentates, are subject to, and must humbly obey.'

Boniface VIII. Extravagant. 'Omnes Christi fideles, &c. It is necessary to salvation that all Christians should be subject to the Roman pontiff.'

Glossa Extrav. Johan. XXII. 'Dominus Deus noster Papa. Our Lord God the Pope.'

Bzovius, de Pontif. Roman. Col. Agrip. cap. 1, 3, 16, 32, and 45. 'Papa est Christianorum Monarcha, &c. The pope is monarch of all Christians. —Supreme over *all* mortals. From him lies no appeal. He is *judge in heaven, and in all earthly jurisdiction supreme : and arbiter of the world*.'

Moscovius, de Majest. Eccles. Militant, lib. 1. cap. 7. page 26. 'Pontifex Romanus est Judex, &c. The pope is universal Judge, *King of kings and Lord of lords*, because his power is of God. God's tribunal and the pope's are the same, and they have the same consistory. All other powers are his subjects. The pope is judged of none but God.'

Mancinus, de Jur. Princip. Rom. lib. 3. cap. 1, 2. 'Papa est totius orbis, &c. The pope is lord of the whole world. The pope, as pope, has temporal power. The pope's temporal power is most eminent. *All other powers depend on the pope*.'

Scioppius, Eccles. Jacob. Mag. Brit. Reg. Oppos. cap. 138, 139, and 241. 'Catholici non tantum Ministerio, &c. The pope's power, as Papists believe, is not only ministerial, but imperial ; and supreme, so that he has the right to direct and compel, with the power of life and death. The pope is the supreme vicar of God ; and the head of Christ's body.'

Maynardus, de Privileg. Eccles. art. 5. sec. 19, 21, 23.; art. 6. sec. 1, 11, 12, 13.; art. 13. sec. 9. 'Emperors and kings are the pope's subjects. Emperors and kings may be deposed by the pope for heresy. The pope has power in the whole world, in spirituals and temporals. The pope is vicar of God, and preferred before all powers, as God himself; and every creature is subject to him. It is necessary to salvation to be subject to the pope, and he who affirms the contrary is no Christian. Statutes made by laymen do not bind the clergy.'

Simanca, Enchir. Judicum, tit. 67. sec. 12. page 349. 'Heretici privati sunt, &c. Heretics are actually deprived of all dominion and jurisdiction, and their subjects are freed from their obedience.'

Emanuel Sa, Aphor. Confes. Verb. Cleric, page 41. 'Clerici rebellio in Regem, &e. If a priest rebel, it is not treason, because clergymen are not the king's subjects.'

Ozichovius, in Chimsera, page 99. 'Sacerdos praestat regi, &c. A priest excels the king, as much as a man excels a beast. He who prefers a king to a priest, prefers the creature before the Creator.'

Corpus Jur. Canonici. Can. Authoritat. 2. Caus. 15. Quest. 6. Part 2. 'A fidelitatis etiam juramento, &c. The pope may depose princes, and absolve their subjects from their oaths of allegiance. The pope does by usual authority so absolve subjects from their oaths to their superiors.' Can. 3.

Turrecremata, Card, ad Can. Alius, 3. Caus. 15. Quest. 6: and de Eccles. lib. 2. cap. 14. 'Papa potest deponere, &c. The pope may depose emperors and kings. The pope may lawfully absolve subjects from their oaths of allegiance. If the king be a manifest heretic, the church may depose him.' "[150]

A state of totalitarian Roman Catholic Integralism under the Papacy is coming and cannot be averted. It is foreordained, as evinced by Bible prophecy. It may take decades for it to be fully established, and this is why they are starting with the children in the schools: conditioning them to the idea of (seemingly) Christian dogmas *coming from the State*.

The Papacy eventually *will* resume carrying out its long-suppressed, yet unchanged, principle of persecuting as heretics any who oppose its views. For each Bible-believing Christian, there remains only a personal choice to be made as to how he or she will face it: whether to succumb or to resist.

"Here is the patience of the saints: here are they that keep the commandments of God, and the faith of Jesus."

—Revelation 14:12 (KJV)

References

[1] HB71 (la.gov) https://www.legis.la.gov/legis/BillInfo.aspx?s=24RS&b=HB71&sbi=y

[2] Louisiana passes law to force classrooms to display The Ten Commandments | Daily Mail Online https://www.dailymail.co.uk/news/article-13548125/Louisiana-law-classrooms-display-Ten-Commandments.html?ci=585594

[3] Louisiana's public classrooms now have to display the Ten Commandments | AP News https://apnews.com/article/louisiana-ten-commandments-displayed-classrooms-571a2447906f7bbd5a166d53db005a62

[4] ibid

[5] 2024 Regular Session HOUSE BILL NO. 71 (la.gov) https://www.legis.la.gov/legis/ViewDocument.aspx?d=1382697

[6] Louisiana's public classrooms now have to display the Ten Commandments | AP News. https://apnews.com/article/louisiana-ten-commandments-displayed-classrooms-

[7] What Is The Main Religion In Louisiana? - CLJ (communityliteracy.org). https://communityliteracy.org/what-is-the-main-religion-in-louisiana/

[8] Louisiana - Culture - Religion (liquisearch.com). https://www.liquisearch.com/louisiana/culture/religion

[9] Louisiana Religion (bestplaces.net). https://www.bestplaces.net/religion/state/louisiana

[10] 2024 Regular Session HOUSE BILL NO. 71 (la.gov). https://www.legis.la.gov/legis/ViewDocument.aspx?d=1382697

[11] U.S. Constitution - First Amendment | Resources | Constitution Annotated | Congress.gov | Library of Congress. https://constitution.congress.gov/constitution/amendment-1/

[12] Supremacy Clause. Wikipedia. https://en.wikipedia.org/wiki/Supremacy_Clause

[13] New Louisiana law requiring classrooms to display Ten Commandments churns old political conflicts | News | register-herald.com. https://www.register-herald.com/news/nation_world/new-louisiana-law-requiring-classrooms-to-display-ten-commandments-churns-old-political-conflicts/article_41d99895-73c7-500d-809b-a482c33f9724.html

[14] Jeff Landry sued over Louisiana Ten Commandments law (lawandcrime.com). https://lawandcrime.com/first-amendment/louisiana-governor-who-said-i-cant-wait-to-be-sued-over-ten-commandments-law-gets-his-wish/

[15] ibid

[16] Founding fathers: God, not religion, was the key (jacksonville.com). https://www.jacksonville.com/story/opinion/letters/2008/12/11/founding-fathers-god-not-religion-was-the-key/16002967007/

[17] The Barbary Treaties 1786-1816 Treaty of Peace and Friendship, Signed at Tripoli November 4, 1796. Avalon.law.yale.edu. https://avalon.law.yale.edu/18th_century/bar1796t.asp

[18] 8 Facts about George Washington and Religion. George Washington's Mount Vernon. https://www.mountvernon.org/george-washington/religion/8-facts-about-george-washington-and-religion/

[19] George Washington and Religion. George Washington's Mount Vernon. https://www.mountvernon.org/library/digitalhistory/digital-encyclopedia/article/george-washington-and-religion/

[20] The 39 Articles Of The Church Of England : David Clarke. https://archive.org/details/39-article-full/page/n7/mode/2up

[21] Thomas Jefferson to Francis Adrian Van der Kemp, 30 July 1816. Founders Online. Founders.archives.gov. https://founders.archives.gov/documents/Jefferson/03-10-02-0167

[22] Why Thomas Jefferson Rewrote the Bible Without Jesus' Miracles and Resurrection | HISTORY. https://www.history.com/news/thomas-jefferson-bible-religious-beliefs

[23] Signers of the Declaration of Independence (ushistory.org). https://www.ushistory.org/declaration/signers/

[24] Rulers of Evil. Useful Knowledge about Governing Bodies. Frederick Tupper Saucy. 1999. Pg. 40. "The Edinburgh lodge would become the headquarters of Scottish Rite Freemasonry, which Masonic historians call "American Freemasonry" because all but five of the signers of the Declaration of Independence are said to have practiced its craft". https://archive.org/details/book-history-jesuits-f.-tupper-saussy-rulers-of-evil/page/39/mode/2up

[25] THE VOLUMES OF THE SACRED LAW (grandlodgeofiowa.org). https://grandlodgeofiowa.org/docs/Freemasonry_Religion/VolumeofSacredLaworiginal.pdf

[26] THREE-GREAT-LIGHTS-OF-MASONRY (freemason.org). https://freemason.org/wp-content/uploads/2020/07/EA-08-THREE-GREAT-LIGHTS-OF-MASONRY.pdf

[27] An Encyclopædia of Freemasonry and Its Kindred Sciences. Volume 1. Albert G. Mackey. 1927. CHICAGO/NEW YORK/LONDON. THE MASONIC HISTORY COMPANY. pg. 104. https://archive.org/details/encyclopaediaoff0001mack/page/104/mode/2up

[28] Occult Theocrasy. Volume 1. Edith Starr Miller. 1933. Pgs. 32-33. https://archive.org/details/occulttheocrasy_201906/page/n29/mode/2up

[29] Pope Francis Decrees That Individual Salvation Outside Of Roman Catholic Church Doesn't Exist. Now The End Begins. https://www.nowtheendbegins.com/pope-francis-decrees-individual-salvation-outside-roman-catholic-church-doesnt-exist/

[30] Catechism Of The Catholic Church. 1129. Internet Archive. https://archive.org/details/CatechismOfTheCatholicChurchUSCCB_201903/Catechism%20Of%20The%20Catholic%20Church/page/n453/mode/2up

[31] Djwhal Khul - The Tibetan - theNewAgeSite. https://www.thenewagesite.com/index.php/articles/alice-a-bailey/djwhal-khul-the-tibetan/

[32] The Esoteric Meaning of Lucifer. Lucis Trust (lucistrust.org). https://www.lucistrust.org/arcane_school/talks_and_articles/the_esoteric_meaning_lucifer

[33] The Secret Doctrine: The Synthesis Science, Religion and Philosophy. 3rd Edition. Volume 2. Anthropogenesis. Helena Blavatsky. 1893.NEW YORK/MADRAS. THE THEOSOPHICAL PUBLISHING SOCIETY. pg. 245 https://archive.org/details/in.ernet.dli.2015.175364/page/n261/mode/2up

[34] THE RETURN OF THE CHRIST - Part 2 - Online Books • Lucis Trust. https://www.lucistrust.org/online_books/the_externalisation_the_hierarchy_obook/the_return_the_christ_part2

[35] The Christ of the New Age Movement. Reasoning From The S (ronrhodes.org). https://www.ronrhodes.org/the-christ-of-the-new-age-movement

[36] SECTION FOUR - STAGES IN THE EXTERNALISATION OF THE HIERARCHY - Part 1 - Online Books • Lucis Trust (lucistrust.org). https://www.lucistrust.org/online_books/the_externalisation_the_hierarchy_obook/section_four_stages_in_the_externalisation_the_hierarchy_part1

[37] Notes on the Bible by Albert Barnes: 1 Corinthians: 1 Corinthians Chapter 5 (sacred-texts.com). https://sacred-texts.com/bib/cmt/barnes/co1005.htm

[38] The Rapture: Fact and Fantasy. My Two Cents. 2023. Draft2Digital. ISBN: 9798223277699. (amazon.com). https://www.amazon.com/Rapture-Fantasy-My-Two-Cents/dp/B0C4G6CH7K

[39] Mandate for Leadership 2025: The Conservative Promise. Heritage Foundation. 2023. pgs. xiii-xiv. (static.project2025.org). https://static.project2025.org/2025_MandateForLeadership_FULL.pdf

[40] Mandate for Leadership 2025: The Conservative Promise. Heritage Foundation. 2023. pg. 589. (static.project2025.org). https://static.project2025.org/2025_MandateForLeadership_FULL.pdf

[41] U.S. Constitution - First Amendment | Resources | Constitution Annotated | Congress.gov | Library of Congress. https://constitution.congress.gov/constitution/amendment-1/

[42] Senate Bill S.2983. 50th Congress, 1st Session..May 21, 1888. Internet Archive. https://archive.org/details/s.-bill-50-2983/mode/2up

[43] in the Greek, ὁ ἄνθρωπος τῆς ἁμαρτίας, literally: "the Man of the Lawlessness". Interlinear breakdown of 2 Thessalonians 2:3. https://biblehub.com/interlinear/2_thessalonians/2-3.htm

[44] Bible Timeline. (biblehub.com). https://biblehub.com/timeline/new.htm

[45] Antiochus IV Epiphanes - Livius. (livius.org). https://www.livius.org/articles/person/antiochus-iv-epiphanes/?

[46] Nero | Biography, Claudius, Rome, Burning, Fate, Accomplishments, & Facts | Britannica. (britannica.com). https://www.britannica.com/biography/Nero-Roman-emperor

[47] Bible Timeline. (biblehub.com). https://biblehub.com/timeline/new.htm

[48] In many Greek source texts, and especially among those of more recent Bible translations, such as that of Westcott & Hort, a definite article ("the") is absent before "antichrist" in 1 John 2:18: ἀντίχριστος ἔρχεται ("antichrist is coming"). However, there it is present in the Greek source texts of the Textus Receptus (Stephanus 1550 & Scrivener's 1894) upon which the King James Version is based, as well as Beza Greek New Testament (1598), Greek Orthodox Church (1904) and RP Byzantine Majority (2005) texts: ὁ ἀντίχριστος ἔρχεται ("the antichrist comes / is coming"). See 1 John 2:18 Greek Text Analysis. https://biblehub.com/text/1_john/2-18.htm

[49] ibid

[50] The Greek word translated in the KJV as "shall come" is ἔρχεται, which is the present indicative middle form, meaning literally "comes" or "is coming" . Interlinear breakdown of 1 John 2:18. https://biblehub.com/interlinear/1_john/2-18.htm

[51] Stephanus Textus Receptus (1550). (biblehub.com). https://biblehub.com/text/1_john/2-18.htm

[52] "As" Definition & Meaning - Merriam-Webster. (meriiam-webster.com). https://www.merriam-webster.com/dictionary/as

[53] Strong's Greek: 2531. καθώς (kathos) -- just as, as. (biblehub.com). https://biblehub.com/greek/2531.htm

[54] The Rapture: Fact and Fantasy. My Two Cents. 2023. Draft2Digital. ISBN: 9798223277699. (amazon.com). https://www.amazon.com/Rapture-Fantasy-My-Two-Cents/dp/B0C4G6CH7K

55 Interlinear Breakdown of Revelation 1:9. (biblehub.com). https://biblehub.com/interlinear/revelation/1-9.htm

56 Interlinear Breakdown of John 16:33. (biblehub.com). https://biblehub.com/interlinear/john/16-33.htm

57 Interlinear Breakdown of Matthew 24:9. (biblehub.com). https://biblehub.com/interlinear/matthew/24-9.htm

58 Foxe's Book of Martyrs. John Foxe. Reproduction. 1563. From Chapter 2. Internet Archive. https://archive.org/details/foxesbookofmartyrs_201708/page/n11/mode/2up

59 Persecution in Lyon. Wikipedia. https://en.wikipedia.org/wiki/Persecution_in_Lyon

60 Persecution of Christians. Wikipedia. https://en.wikipedia.org/wiki/Persecution_of_Christians

61 ibid.

62 ibid.

63 ibid.

64 Marx & Satan. Richard Wurmbrand. 1986. Sixth Printing. 1990. Westchester, IL. Crossway Books. pg. 74. *Archive.org*. https://ia601807.us.archive.org/18/items/marx-and-satan-richard-wurmbrandt/Marx_and_Satan_Richard_Wurmbrandt.pdf

65 Persecution of Christians. Wikipedia. https://en.wikipedia.org/wiki/Persecution_of_Christians

66 World Watch List 2023. *Opendoors.org*. https://www.opendoors.org/en-US/persecution/countries/

67 Christians will face jail in Israel for proselytising under proposed bill. *Middleeastmonitor.com*. https://www.middleeastmonitor.com/20230322-christians-will-face-jail-in-israel-for-proselytising-under-proposed-bill/

68 The Rapture: Fact and Fantasy. My Two Cents. 2023. Draft2Digital. ISBN: 9798223277699. Chapter 12, "We are Not Appointed to Wrath". https://www.amazon.com/Rapture-Fantasy-My-Two-Cents/dp/B0C4G6CH7K

69 Reformation Papacy. *Wikipedia*. https://en.wikipedia.org/wiki/Reformation_Papacy

70 Estimates of the Number Killed by The Papacy in the Middle Ages and Later. *Static1.1.sqspcdn.com*. David A. Plaisted. http://static1.1.sqspcdn.com/static/f/827989/15116787/1321289366180/50+million+protestants+killed.pdf

71 The Rapture: Fact and Fantasy. My Two Cents. 2023. Draft2Digital. ISBN: 9798223277699. https://www.amazon.com/Rapture-Fantasy-My-Two-Cents/dp/B0C4G6CH7K

72 Protestant Reformation - World History Encyclopedia (worldhistory.org). https://www.worldhistory.org/Protestant_Reformation/

73 Explanatory notes upon the New Testament. John Wesley. 12th Edition. 1754. NEW YORK. CARLTON & PORTER. pg. 704. Internet Archive. https://archive.org/details/explanatorynotes00unknuoft/page/n709/mode/2up

74 The Rapture: Fact and Fantasy. My Two Cents. 2023. Draft2Digital. ISBN: 9798223277699. Chapter 10 "The Absence of the Church in Revelation Chapters 4-18" https://www.amazon.com/Rapture-Fantasy-My-Two-Cents/dp/B0C4G6CH7K

75 ibid

76 The People's Edition of the Westminster Confession of Faith. John Macpherson. 1881. MELBOURNE. M. L. HUTCHINSON, PRESBYTERIAN BOOK DEPOT. pg. 13. Internet Archive. https://archive.org/details/westminsterconfe00macp/page/144/mode/2up

77 Smalcald Articles. Archived from bookofconcord.org. Internet Archive Wayback Machine (web.archive.org). https://web.archive.org/web/20080829021137/http://www.bookofconcord.org/smalcald.html#article4

78 1689 Baptist Confession. (apuritansmind.com). https://www.apuritansmind.com/creeds-and-confessions/1689-baptist-confession/

79 Overture on Revision; Answers of the Presbyteries. Presbyterian Church in the U.S.A. 1890. CINCINNATI. General Assembly. pg. 21. Internet Archive. https://archive.org/details/overtureonrevisi00pres/page/20/mode/2up

80 How shall we revise the Westminster confession of faith?. Llewellyn J. Evans, *et al.* 1890. NEW YORK. CHARLES SCRIBNER'S SONS. pg. 149. Internet Archive. https://archive.org/details/howshallwerevise00evan/page/148/mode/2up

81 Prompta Bibliotheca Canonica, Juridica, Moralis, Theologica. Ac in Octo Tomos Distributa (Distributed in Eight Volumes). Tomus Sextus P=R (Volume Six, "P" through "R"). Lucius Ferraris. 1772. VENETIIS (VENICE). GASPAREM STORTI (GASPARE STORTI)). See "Papa, Articulus II, Quo ad ea, quæ concernant Papæ dignitatem, auctoritatem, seu potestatem, & infallibilitatem". pg. 27. *"Sanctam Romanam Ecclesiam, et Te Rectorem ipsius exaltabo; cap. Constantinus 14. diat. 96. ibi; Ut sicut Beatus Petrus in terris Vicarius Filii Dei fuit constitutus, ita et Pontifices ejus Successores in terris principatus potestatem amplius, quam terrenae Imperialis nostrae serenitatis mansuetudo habere videtur"*. Internet Archive. https://archive.org/details/bub_gb_M42pO2ofQaAC/page/26/mode/2up

82 Senate Committee Hearing, Sunday Rest Bill. U.S. Senate. 50th Congress. 2nd Session. Dec. 13, 1888. Mis. Doc. No. 43. Ordered to be printed Jan. 17, 1889. pg. 18. Internet Archive. https://archive.org/details/senate-committee-hearing-sunday-rest-bill/page/18/mode/2up

83 Senate Bill S.2983. 50th Congress, 1st Session..May 21, 1888. Internet Archive. https://archive.org/details/s.-bill-50-2983/mode/2up

[84] Senate Committee Hearing, Sunday Rest Bill. Senate. 50th Congress. 2nd Session. Dec. 13, 1888. Mis. Doc. No. 43. Ordered to be printed Jan. 17, 1889. pg. 18. Internet Archive. https://archive.org/details/senate-committee-hearing-sunday-rest-bill/page/18/mode/2up

[85] Catechism Of The Catholic Church. 2089. Internet Archive https://archive.org/details/CatechismOfTheCatholicChurchUSCCB_201903/Catechism%20Of%20The%20Catholic%20Church/page/n763/mode/2up

[86] Heresy (Defined by Roman Catholicism). Internet Archive https://archive.org/details/heresy_202306/page/n5/mode/2up

[87] Directory for the Application of the Decisions of the Second Ecumenical Council of the Vatican Concerning Ecumenical Matters, May 14, 1967, Part I : Catholic Church. Secretariatus ad Christianorum Unitatem Fovendam. 1967. pg. 20. Internet Archive https://archive.org/details/directoryforappl00cath/page/n1/mode/2up

[88] Facts Of Faith. Christian Edwardson. 1943. Southern Publishing Assn. pg. 292. "Had she not such power, she could not have done that in which all modern religionists agree with her;—she could not have substituted the observance of Sunday, the first day of the week, for the observance of Saturday, the seventh day, a change for which there is no Scriptural authority."— 'Doctrinal Catechism,' p. 174. New York: P. J. Kenedy and Sons , 1846." Internet Archive. https://archive.org/details/EdwardsonFactsOfFaith1943SouthernPublishing/page/n293/mode/2up

[89] Liberty. 1907. Vol 2 Iss. 3. pgs. 22-23. Internet Archive https://archive.org/details/sim_liberty_1907_2_3/page/22/mode/2up

[90] Luis del Alcázar. Wikipedia. https://en.wikipedia.org/wiki/Luis_del_Alc%C3%A1zar

[91] Francisco Ribera. Wikipedia. https://en.wikipedia.org/wiki/Francisco_Ribera

[92] The Rapture: Fact and Fantasy. My Two Cents. 2023. Draft2Digital. ISBN: 9798223277699. https://www.amazon.com/Rapture-Fantasy-My-Two-Cents/dp/B0C4G6CH7K

[93] Edward Irving: An Ecclesiastical and Literary Biography. Washington Wilks. 1854. LONDON. WILLIAM FREEMAN. pg. 273. Internet Archive https://archive.org/details/edwardirvingane02wilkgoog/page/n284/mode/2up

[94] Manuel Lacunza. Wikipedia. https://en.wikipedia.org/wiki/Manuel_Lacunza

[95] Edward Irving: An Ecclesiastical and Literary Biography. Washington Wilks. 1854. LONDON. WILLIAM FREEMAN. pg. 273. Internet Archive https://archive.org/details/edwardirvingane02wilkgoog/page/n284/mode/2up

[96] The Prophetic Faith Of Our Fathers. Vol. 4. Le Roy Edwin Froom. 1954. WASHINGTON, D.C. Review and Herald. pg. 420. Internet Archive. https://archive.org/details/prophecy-le-roy-edwin-froom-prophetic-faith-of-our-fathers-04-pfof-1954-v-04_20230114/page/420/mode/2up

[97] ibid. pg. 1226

[98] ibid. pg. 1203

[99] Mystery Babylon The Great. Vol. 2. I.A. Sadler. CHIPPENHAM, U.K. 2014. pg. 34. Internet Archive. https://archive.org/details/sadler-i.-a.-mystery-babylon-the-great-vol.-1/Sadler%20I.A.%20-%20Mystery%20Babylon%20the%20Great%20Vol.%202/page/34/mode/2up

[100] Plain Talk about the Protestantism of To-Day. Mgr. De Ségur (Louis Gaston). 1868. BOSTON: Patrick Donahoe. pg. 225. Internet Archive. https://archive.org/details/PlainTalkAboutTheProtestantism/page/n229/mode/2up

[101] The Catholic Record. Sept. 1, 1923. "SABBATH OBSERVANCE". LONDON, ON. pg. 4. Archive.org. https://archive.org/details/catholic-record-full/page/n3/mode/2up

[102] Facts Of Faith. Christian Edwardson. 1943. NASHVILLE. Southern Publishing Assn. pgs. 292-293. Internet Archive https://archive.org/details/EdwardsonFactsOfFaith1943SouthernPublishing/page/n293/mode/2up

[103] The Catechism Simply Explained (romerules.com). Henry T. Cafferata. 1935. https://www.romerules.com/the-catechism-simply-explained.html

[104] Secrets Unsealed: The Great Prophecies Of Daniel & Revelation. Stephen Bohr. pg. 221. Internet Archive https://archive.org/details/secrets-unsealed-stephen-bohr-the-great-prophecies-of-daniel-revelation/page/220/mode/2up

[105] The Christian Sabbath: Is it Saturday or Sunday? A Careful Study of this Important Religious Question from the Standpoint of the Scriptures of Truth. Carlyle B. Haynes. 1916. FORT WORTH/ATLANTA. SOUTHERN PUBLISHING ASSN. pg. 78. Internet Archive https://archive.org/details/CarlyleB.HaynesTheChristianSabbath.IsItSaturdayOrSundayACareful/page/n77/mode/2up

[106] Palm Springs Desert Sun (1951-04-27). Internet Archive. https://archive.org/details/palm-springs-desert-sun-1951-04-27/page/n7/mode/2up

[107] Ukiah Republican Press (1914-07-24). Internet Archive. https://archive.org/details/ukiah-republican-press-1914-07-24/page/n3/mode/2up

[108] Experiences of a Pioneer Minister of Minnesota. William B. Hill. 1892. MINNEAPOLIS. PRESS OF J.A. FOLSOM. pg. 96. Internet Archive. https://archive.org/details/cu31924029459553/page/n101/mode/2up

[109] The Lord's Day from Neither Catholics Nor Pagans. 2nd Edition. Dudley Marvin Canright. 1915. NEW YORK. FLEMING H. REVELL CO. pg. 74. Internet Archive. https://archive.org/details/lordsdayfromneit00canr/page/74/mode/2up

[110] Council of Laodicea - Wikipedia. https://en.wikipedia.org/wiki/Council_of_Laodicea

[111] Third Council of Orléans - Wikipedia. https://en.wikipedia.org/wiki/Third_Council_of_Orl%C3%A9ans

[112] Experiences of a Pioneer Minister of Minnesota. William B. Hill. 1892. MINNEAPOLIS. PRESS OF J.A. FOLSOM. pg. 92. Internet Archive. https://archive.org/details/cu31924029459553/page/n97/mode/2up

[113] In 1 John 3:4, in the King James Version, the Greek word translated as "transgression of the law" is "ἀνομία" ("lawlessness", per Strong's Concordance #458: https://biblehub.com/greek/458.htm)

[114] Catechism Of The Catholic Church. "SABBATH". Internet Archive https://archive.org/details/CatechismOfTheCatholicChurchUSCCB_201903/Catechism%20Of%20The%20Catholic%20Church/page/n1559/mode/2up

[115] The Baptist Catechism: Commonly Called Keach's Catechism. 1851. PHILADELPHIA. AMERICAN BAPTIST PUBLICATION SOCIETY. pg. 19. Internet Archive. https://archive.org/details/MN40248ucmf_4/page/n19/mode/2up

[116] The Westminster Shorter Catechism: With Analysis, Scriptural Proofs. James Robert Boyd. 1956. NEW YORK. M. W. DODD. pgs. 146-147. Internet Archive. https://archive.org/details/westminstershor00boydgoog/page/n154/mode/2up

[117] The Heidelberg Catechism. 1879.TIFFIN, OH. H. R. GOOD & BRO. pgs. 65-66. Internet Archive. https://archive.org/details/heidelbergcatech00refo/page/64/mode/2up

[118] Luther's Small Catechism. Martin Luther. Translation. Evangelical Lutheran Synod of Pennsylvania. 1863. PHILADELPHIA. G. W. FREDERICK. pgs. 31-32. Internet Archive. https://archive.org/details/lutherssmallcate00luth_0/page/30/mode/2up

[119] Exodus 20:10 Interlinear (biblehub.com). https://biblehub.com/interlinear/exodus/20-10.htm

[120] A General History of the Sabbatarian Churches: Embracing Accounts of the Armenian, East Indian, and Abyssinian Episcopacies in Asia and Africa, the Waldenses, Semi-Judaisers, and Sabbatarian Anabaptists of Europe, with the Seventh-Day Baptist Denomination in the United States. Tamar Davis. 1851. PHILADELPHIA. LINDSAY AND BLAKISTON. pgs. ix-x. Internet Archive. https://archive.org/details/generalhistoryo00davi/page/n7/mode/2up

[121] Apollon. Theoi.com. 4/8/2023 https://www.theoi.com/Olympios/Apollon.html

[122] UNIVERSITY STUDIES, Vol. XI, JANUARY-APRIL, Nos. 1-2. Rest Days; A Sociological Study. Hutton Webster. 1911. Lincoln. University of Nebraska. pg. 61. Internet Archive. https://archive.org/details/restdayssociolog0000webs/page/60/mode/2up

[123] Ecclesiastical Empire. Alonzo T. Jones. 1901. REVIEW AND HERALD PUBLISHING CO. BATTLE CREEK, MI. pg. 263. Internet Archive. "…Eostre, Ostâra, Ishtar, Astarte, Ashtaroth, — the female element in sun worship." https://archive.org/details/ecclesiastical-empire-1901-review-and-herald/page/n145/mode/2up

[124] Artemis. Wikipedia. https://en.wikipedia.org/wiki/Artemis

[125] Astarte | Phoenician goddess, Canaanite goddess, fertility goddess | Britannica (brittanica.com). https://www.britannica.com/topic/Astarte-ancient-deity

[126] Records Of The Past: Ancient Monuments of Egypt & Western Asia. Vol. IX. Assyrian Texts. A H. Sayce. 1877. LONDON. SAMUEL BAGSTER AND SONS. pg. 96. Internet Archive. "May ISTAR, the Queen of heaven and earth, carry him off, and deliver him for avenge to the god and the king." https://archive.org/details/SayceAHRecordsOfThePastVol09AncientMonumentsOfEgyptWesternAsia/page/n107/mode/2up

[127] The Secret Teachings Of All Ages - Manly P Hall. 1928. SAN FRANCISCO. H.S. CROCKER CO. INC. pg. 46. Internet Archive. "ISIS, QUEEN OF HEAVEN". https://archive.org/details/The_Secret_Teachings_Of_All_Ages_-_Manly_P_Hall/page/n97/mode/2up

[128] Cyclopedia Of Biblical Literature. Vol. 2. John Kitto. 1845. EDINBURGH. ADAM AND CHARLES BLACK. pgs. 356-357. Internet Archive. "MOON". https://archive.org/details/CyclopediaOfBiblicalLiteratureEdJohnKittoVol21845/page/n365/mode/2up

[129] The Catechism Simply Explained (romerules.com). Images of book pages. Henry T. Cafferata. 1935. https://www.romerules.com/the-catechism-simply-explained.html

[130] The Controversy Between Senator Brooks and "John," Archbishop of New York Growing Out of the Speech of Senator Brooks on the Church Property Bill, in the N. Y. State Senate, March 6th, 1855. Eratus Brooks. 1855. NEW YORK. DE WITT & DAVENPORT. pg. 18. https://archive.org/details/controversybetwe00broo/page/18/mode/2up

[131] Laudato si' (24 May 2015) | Francis (vatican.va) https://www.vatican.va/content/francesco/en/encyclicals/documents/papa-francesco_20150524_enciclica-laudato-si.html#_ftnref1

[132] Thayer's Greek Lexicon: "ἐπί". See definition "A.I.1.d) d. figuratively used of things, affairs, persons, which one is set over, over which he exercises power". https://biblehub.com/greek/1909.htm

[133] Banias - Wikipedia https://en.wikipedia.org/wiki/Banias

[134] The World Factbook: Syria. https://www.cia.gov/the-world-factbook/countries/syria/

[135] The Book of Enoch the Prophet. Richard Laurence. 1883. LONDON. KEGAN PAUL, TRENCH & CO. pg. 6. Internet Archive. https://archive.org/details/cu31924090062823/page/n61/mode/2up

[136] Strong's Concordance: "καί". See "Usage: and, even, also, namely.". https://biblehub.com/greek/2532.htm

[137] Laudato si' (24 May 2015) | Francis (vatican.va) https://www.vatican.va/content/francesco/en/encyclicals/documents/papa-francesco_20150524_enciclica-laudato-si.html#_ftnref1

[138] *The Satanic Aim of the United Nations, World Economic Forum & Great Reset*. My Two Cents | Goodreads. The original eBook and paperback editions of this title, which were first published in 2022 via Amazon distribution, are no longer available on Amazon. Amazon shut down the author's publishing account on February 8th, 2023 and refused to pay the author's accrued royalties, based on a vaguely-worded claim that the author had violated its terms of service. Amazon refused repeated requests to provide a clear explanation as to what term(s) the author had allegedly violated. However, the mass-market paperback, released by the author in February 2023 through another publishing agent, is now sold on Amazon by third-party retailers, and it and the reissued eBook are now available on many more online retailers than previously. https://www.goodreads.com/book/show/91293200-the-satanic-aim-of-the-united-nations-world-economic-forum-great-rese

[139] The Satanic Aim of the United Nations, World Economic Forum & Great Reset: Amazon.com. My Two Cents: ISBN 9798215957462. https://www.amazon.com/Satanic-United-Nations-World-Economic/dp/B0BS921MPC

[140] God Bless the U.S.A. Bible - Wikipedia. https://en.wikipedia.org/wiki/God_Bless_the_U.S.A._Bible

[141] Mirari Vos - Papal Encyclicals. https://www.papalencyclicals.net//greg16/g16mirar.htm

[142] Inter Praecipuas - Papal Encyclicals. https://www.papalencyclicals.net/greg16/g16inter.htm

[143] Establishment Clause | Wex | US Law | LII / Legal Information Institute (cornell.edu) https://www.law.cornell.edu/wex/establishment_clause

[144] Lauren Boebert Says the Church Is Supposed To Direct the Government - Newsweek. https://www.newsweek.com/lauren-boebert-church-founding-fathers-government-colorado-1719760

[145] Jefferson's Letter to the Danbury Baptists (June 1998) - Library of Congress Information Bulletin (loc.gov) https://www.loc.gov/loc/lcib/9806/danpost.html

[146] 'A Wall of Separation' (June 1998) - Library of Congress Information Bulletin (loc.gov) "The text as recovered by the FBI Laboratory shows that Jefferson first wrote 'a wall of eternal separation.' ". https://www.loc.gov/loc/lcib/9806/danbury.html

[147] Foxe's Book of Martyrs. John Foxe. Reproduction. 1563. From Chapter 4. Internet Archive. https://archive.org/details/foxesbookofmartyrs_201708/page/n89/mode/2up

[148] Estimates of the Number Killed by The Papacy in the Middle Ages and Later. David A. Plaisted. 2006. Static1.1.sqspcdn.com. http://static1.1.sqspcdn.com/static/f/827989/15116787/1321289366180/50+million+protestants+killed.pdf

[149] Foreign Conspiracy Against the Liberties of the United States: The Numbers of Brutus. Samuel Finley Breese Morse. 1835. NEW YORK. LEAVITT, LORD & CO./G. & C. CARVILL & CO. | BOSTON. CROCKER & BREWSTER. pgs. 57-59. Internet Archive. https://archive.org/details/foreignconspiracy00morsrich/page/56/mode/2up

[150] The Protestant: Essays on the Principal Points of Controversy between the Church of Rome and the Reformed. Vol. II. William McGavin. 1834. HARTFORD. HUTCHISON AND DWIER. pgs. 683-685. Internet Archive. https://archive.org/details/protestantessays0002mgav/page/682/mode/2up